I0756437

FEARLESS PERSISTENCE

CREATIVE LIFE, CREATIVE WORK, AND THE TEN LAWS OF CULTURENOMICS

YOUR GUIDE TO PRACTICE AND PHILOSOPHY

ADAM LEIPZIG

Printed in the United States of America.

For more information or to book a workshop, training, retreat, or event, contact :

adam@adamleipzig.com
https://www.adamleipzig.com

Book design by Honeylette Pino
Cover design by Oliver Munday

ISBN Paperback: 978-0-9885342-4-7
ISBN Hardcover: 978-0-9885342-3-0
ISBN Kindle: 978-0-9885342-5-4

First Edition: April 2026

DISCLAIMER

This book shares stories, insights, and lessons from my own creative life and the experiences of people I've worked with. Along the way, I talk about legal issues, business structures, finances, taxes, contracts, negotiations, and other real-world matters. I do this because creative life doesn't happen in a vacuum: it happens in the world, with all its practical details.

But I want to be absolutely clear: Nothing in this book is legal, financial, tax, or professional advice. Nor does this book create a fiduciary relationship between us. I am not your attorney, accountant, tax advisor, financial planner, therapist, or professional consultant. I'm a storyteller and a guide, sharing what has worked for me and others, *not* giving instructions for what you should do.

Every creative path is different, as are the laws and regulations in different states and countries. Before making decisions about your business, finances, legal rights, tax status, investments, creative works, intellectual property, or anything that could affect your livelihood or well-being, you should seek advice from licensed professionals who understand your specific situation.

Nothing in this book creates any kind of client relationship. Nothing here should be relied upon as a substitute for expert guidance. If you take an action based on something I've described, you do so at your own risk.

My goal is to inspire you, encourage you, and help you think more boldly and more creatively about your work and your life. Use these ideas as sparks. Then, as in all of your creative journey, make your own informed decisions with the right professional support at your side.

CONTENTS

PART ONE: FUNDAMENTALS FOR HEART AND MIND

PART TWO:
CREATIVE LIFE PRACTICUM

PART THREE: THE TEN LAWS OF CULTURENOMICS

PREFACE
YOUR BOLD STEP

Congratulations! You have just taken a bold step toward expanding your creative powers. You hold in your hands a guidebook for your creative acts.

This guidebook will make your creative work stronger and better, and will help you bring it to your audience.

You will have to be fearless, even when fear eats your desire. You will have to persist, even when ceasing would allow you to breathe with grateful relief.

If you're reading this book, you're a creative person. As a creative person, you've probably been doing your work for some time, and you already have your own way of doing it. You might even say that the way you work now is your personal guidebook, although you may not have realized it, and you probably didn't call it that. Your personal guidebook is already tremendous and has a lot of value for you. It is comprised of the ways you have been dreaming, doing, crafting, creating, and working, including the times you have not been working, and it also contains the workarounds you devised when some things seemed too complicated or laborious or you just didn't feel like you wanted to do them.

You will find that this guidebook complements yours and will give you some new ideas about how to operate. Why? When you were creating your own personal way of working, you probably did not think about it methodically; you probably just wanted to get right to it, or you slowly discovered you were doing your work and you have not examined how it's going and if it could be improved.

Here's an example. Much of the time, we go to our known shortcuts and quick-starts. All kinds of hacks and prompts might get you better results, but unless you really take the time to explore them, you will never know about them—even if knowing about them would make your work much easier because it would let you do something in one step instead of five.

I'm not sure about the idea of a creative guidebook. Doesn't creativity get ruined when you try to define it?

In many ways, you're right. I don't believe that creative work is the same from person to person or work to work, and neither do you. But this guidebook will help creative people in a lot of ways. You will find at least one idea or workflow that fundamentally transforms the way you make your work and make your living from it.

So, how do I use this guidebook?

Skip around if you want. Use it in a way that is practical for you.

I'm comfortable with that.

This book is in three big sections. They are:

- **Fundamentals for Heart and Mind.** This is the section you're about to start. It's about philosophy, motivation, emotions and mindset, why you do what you do.
- **Creative Life Practicum.** These are the details you need to pay attention to, because if you don't they will come around and bite you. Others require you to take actions to ensure your creativity is well-positioned for the future.

- **The Ten Laws of Culturenomics.** When your creative spirit and your creative practice meet, you will be living the Creative Life. This Life has a unique set of Laws that govern how creative work is shared among its audiences. Learning and following these Ten Laws will become the spiritual and financial core of your success.

That all sounds pretty definitive. What makes you so expert that you can write this book?

Thanks for calling me an "expert," but here's what it feels like: Every day I wake up blurry with uncertainty, and every night I go to sleep wondering if I did all I could do during the day. Really, I'm just like you. The one way that I may be different is that I've worked with more than ten thousand creative people in my career in film, theater, entrepreneurship, and business. I've been studying the creative process for a long time, and I have observed what works for many people like you, including people who may already be more advanced in their careers. I frequently get requests to share the information I have gathered, so I have put it together here.

I began my career in theater, first at the Los Angeles Actors' Theatre, and then as part of the team that built and opened the Los Angeles Theatre Center, a four-theater performing arts complex in downtown Los Angeles. We produced primarily new plays, and also music, dance, poetry, and performance art events.

Then I transitioned to Disney, my big job at a movie studio. When I began, Disney was—I kid you not—a smallish company that had not had much success. Our creative team was eight people, with me the most junior. This meant we needed to do a lot of work and make a bunch of movies. I made fifteen films while I was there.

By that time, Disney had grown, I had been promoted up so far that when I went to visit a film in production people would call out the warning, "Suit on the set!" Ugh. That wasn't why I got into film. So I quit and became a producer, first for independent companies and then on my own.

The National Geographic Society had been curious about the movie business; they asked me to write a strategic plan for them, then asked me to run the company. I was president of National Geographic Films for seven years; that's when I started adding documentaries to my filmmaking repertoire.

After my time at Nat Geo came to a close, Macmillan's educational imprint asked me to be the lead author on a new, definitive college filmmaking textbook. This led me to teaching, first in film school and, now, for the past dozen years, at the Haas School of Business at UC Berkeley. I don't teach film there—I teach business communications to MBA students, senior executives, business leaders, the biggest tech companies in the world, and international government officials. Through my interactions with these remarkable individuals, I have deepened the fusion of business expertise with the creative impulse, a personal bridge-making that has led me here.

This book is the distillation of what I have learned, discovered, and observed over nearly four decades of creative work. It contains essential truths, not ephemeral trends that expire quickly. But writing this book has posed a special challenge, because, on the one hand, I want to be clear and definitive enough to give you specific actions you can take, and, on the other hand, not all actions work for all people and much of creativity involves no action at all: At times, creativity is the still, humble, vulnerable opening that allows an inflow of inspiration. So I hope this book is primarily a conversation—between me and you; actually, between you and yourself.

What's the big picture?

When you create, you are making something and you own it. Even if your experience of creativity is that you are a vessel, that an outside creative force sweeps through you and moves your fingers, the outcome is one you must claim. That claim is what will allow you to make a sustainable life for yourself, and not shunt your creative efforts aside as mere hobbies. You own, and are responsible for, your creativity: the process, not just the product. You have a responsibility to yourself to use and share your creative energies, and a responsibility to others, knowing that your work affects the world. This guidebook provides pathways for all of that.

Sound good?

Yeah, I think so.

Great. Let's get started!

PART ONE

FUNDAMENTALS FOR HEART AND MIND

1

INEVITABILITY AND ITS PATHWAYS

You have no choice but to express yourself as you do—in books or media, organizational development or music, visual art or video, disruptive technologies or design. If you had a choice, you would have chosen something else, because the work you do is sometimes hard, but you keep coming back to it, with the recognition that this is just who you are.

You've achieved some success or praise from trusted, objective people, so you know you're not fooling yourself, you know that you actually can produce good work, even though the possibility that you may be fooling yourself, that you will never achieve the cultural impact and commercial success of your imagination, still gnaws. (Even outwardly successful people feel this gut-gnaw of doubt.) You may see others having financial outcomes you wish you had, and you realize that no one will do this for you but you. That's what makes you an entrepreneur.

You can launch a start-up, write a book, direct a movie, compose a song, engineer a prompt, shoot a photo, inspire your enterprise, craft your art.

So what?

If it were as easy as getting a payment app for your smartphone and asking people to tap, your problems would be solved. But it is not that easy. Because, when you look around, there are and have been no obvious precedents for your path.

This is the dilemma creative people face; it is amplified because we often feel alone. We work in small groups, in studios or start-ups, or privately, in coffee shops, or at home, or at night away from our "day jobs." So we feel we need to *invent* the path to success even as we engage in the journey. How do we discover the path? We seek other people's stories.

Their journeys inspire us, and I'll recount some of them in this book, but they can also seem distant from the circumstances of our own lives. That's because we don't have enough information to break them down and discover what would be practical for us.

Forging your creative journey, despite its rigors, can be thrilling, because you will discover how to blaze your own trail.

But sometimes it's completely discouraging, so impossible. I find myself just wanting to put it away, stop, do something else, something easier. End this frustrating part of my life.

Hey, you've got to keep going. I know sometimes you want to stop, but the stop is really more of a pause, isn't it, because the going is the path. Don't stray.

Maybe… But what if there isn't a path?

2

HERE IS A STORY

Every tradition has a version of this story, which is your story, too.

It is a story about heroes, although they start out very much like you and me. They came from unexceptional beginnings and at first did not want to be heroic at all. Although they dreamed. They dreamed of lofty things, and because of that they sometimes appeared to others as strange, impractical and even antisocial. Sometimes their shyness looked like arrogance, but really, they were just insecure and felt more comfortable when set apart from others.

In time, though, the heroes were called to their task, and it was the stuff of legend. Really. They went on a journey and battled enormous obstacles—marauding armies, fire-spewing dragons, treacherous landscapes. They faced dark hours and almost failed. In that failure, a part of themselves died, the part that had been encumbered by self-doubt and shame, and they got back on their feet and succeeded. Poems have been penned about them, songs sung, novels written, and these heroes are featured in many of our movies. When we hear these stories, and we do hear them, again and again, we feel at once connected and removed—removed because we do not have actual superpowers, and connected, because we want to have them. The heroes' aspiration is our own aspiration. We breathe that every day.

We are all heroes, or want to be. The problem is that the hero's journey as depicted in movies or books or poems, even as depicted in the autobiographies of others, does not apply to many of us. We don't live in the wasteland, never get called on a formal quest, never seize the sword in the stone, never return to heal the kingdom, make the desert verdant, or marry into a royal family.

Our hero's journey—the journey of the 21st-century Creative Life—is different. We're not always certain that we hear the voice calling us. We try a lot and fail a lot. When we have success, it is often fleeting, and we rarely see vast systemic change as the result of our actions.

Our hero's journey is quieter, more subtle, and often more inward-focused. There are times when we retreat from acclaim; our usual recourse is to hide from what we have accomplished.

Even the most famous and productive among us experience this inward focus.

If we were to feel deeply within ourselves, we would recognize that creativity is the wellspring for all innovation, human expression, and stories. It is the font of all discoveries and new research. It is the birthplace of ideas and dreams, of culture and art, and the promise of our future.

In our contemporary world, so far from the mythic past, we walk the stones of creativity's path. But we rarely understand where we put our feet, or that we tread on a path made by others.

That doesn't feel very satisfying.

Well, that's how the story goes. The text is the text, and it tells you a few things, but not everything. To understand everything, the text must be read by an enlightened person—at which point the letters burst to fire, and the true meaning of the text reveals itself in flame.

You might have to read that last paragraph out loud, see how it feels.

Signifying?

You are a sacred text, your creativity is the fire. It is what you aspire to, and what illuminates your path. It shines a light and attracts others to you.

I'm not sure about any of this. You jump right into big stuff. How about a bit more preparation beforehand?

3

WHAT YOU DO MATTERS

Even at the moment you were born, you were in the middle of things. There is never a time you're not. You've got to keep going.

Because what you do matters.

There are eight billion people in the world, I'm only one of them, so I'm one eight-billionth, less than microscopic.

It isn't so much about the numbers, because creativity isn't data science. The world we live in, our societies, our communities, so often are places of confusion. Anger abounds. Inequality stares us in the face. Violence, physical and political, intimidates us. Deep injustice maims those on whom it is inflicted and, whether we acknowledge it or not, all of us.

It is so much easier to destroy than to create. So much easier to take a life than to make one.

To write a book, build a building, compose a song can take years of going forward and back, marrying and divorcing collaborators, trying versions that disappoint and trying again, passing through the portals of regulators and gatekeepers. Yet, in seconds, a match, a bomb, a corrupted hard drive will eradicate it all.

What we observe seems so asymmetric: our brushes, cadenzas, and keystrokes versus their politics, militaries, and structures. Follow this thought through to the end and any person's creative activity seems small and hopeless.

Why, indeed, do we do it? Why don't we just give up, stop?

Because, as we burrow into it, as you dive deep into your soul, you recognize just the opposite. That suicidal impulse—that's what we're witnessing in society at large. Vilification of the other, racism, militarism, data secrecy, unaccountable corporate actions, corruption, factionalism, violence, economic segregation. The list stretches to the horizon. These are the signs of civilization taking its own life, blood-drop by blood-drop. Throughout history, civilizations have not spontaneously extinguished; they have collapsed of self-inflicted wounds, suicided by themselves through a thousand schisms.

So why do we do what we do?

Because we perceive this.

Your art, your creative work, is the antidote. Each word you type, line you draw, purposefully made, purposefully directed, is salve to worldly wounds.

What you do matters because it makes meaning—your meaning and meaning for us all. The antidote to violence is caring. The antidote to despair is hope. The antidote to hopelessness is purpose.

The purpose of your work is to cultivate an environment where we can all detect our purpose.

Without the brave actions of creative people, civic meaning falls away like leaves from a tree in winter.

You talk about being brave. Sometimes it feels like we are up against the impossible.

4

THE IRON FIST, THE BROKEN HAND

It can feel like we are standing in front of a towering, elemental wall. How can we, with our poor hands, our meager craft, do anything in the face of it?

And when that wall crashes down on us, as it does sometimes—because of big companies citing their contracts, governments enacting and enforcing oppressive laws—some of us crumble, some of us break.

But think about this. Why do some governments put poets in jail? Maybe you are a poet, or maybe you have met one. Poets are not threatening. They're nice people to have dinner with. Half of them don't even talk that much. But words matter, words have power, and the words of some poets can topple regimes. Which is why some poets are in jails right now.

The iron fist comes down to break the poet's hand.

That elemental wall facing us has tremendous scale, it is large and deep. It "scales" as a verb, too, scales as a business does, increasing its operating size and efficiency, becoming more powerful as it expands.

Meanwhile, our work, the work of Creative Life, is based on finite acts of love, trust, compassion. Our work seems not to scale well because it is based on individual actions and relationships.

Yet: We who live Creative Life know how to scale the most powerful force, which is Empathy.

Repeat this to yourself every day: We Scale Empathy and Therefore Scale Transformation.

It takes a broken hand to mend a broken world.

Transformation? But what if I'm not trying to change the world?

5

YOU ARE HERE NOW

Look around you. I mean really look. Not at your phone, not at your custom-skinned carefully tailored news feed. Look at the currents beneath. We are living through days when friends unfriend each other over beliefs, when people gather in groups to shout their rage, when some swing fists or worse because they believe the fight is worth more than the conversation. Borders are shifting, alliances fracture, old empires once again unsheathe their weapons.

If you have grown up in America, you have been feeling the undertow for some years. Now you feel the structures of an empire coming undone, inside and out. The future is uncertain: Will structures break apart or hold?

And you, my friend, were born into this. You did not ask for this moment in history, but you are part of it whether you like it or not. Some nights you may wish you could slip backward in time or leap ahead to a more sensible age. But no other age wants you. This one does.

You are here now. You have a purpose that no law can outlaw, no decree can erase. Your purpose is not to out-shout your neighbors on social media. Your purpose is stranger, quieter, more dangerous than that.

You are here to dream. To create. To weave images and words and sounds and shapes into the stories we need—stories that hold up a mirror to our brokenness and show us a better reflection of who we could become.

Is that enough?

Yes. It has always been enough. More than enough.

People say art does not change the world. They are wrong. Everything around you—every right you enjoy, every freedom you lean on—exists because a story made it possible. Stories shape the beliefs that shape our institutions, our laws, our revolutions, our reconciliations.

Your work is not a hobby to soothe yourself while the world burns. Your work is an ember blown from mind to mind, a reminder that we can still share a common language of fairness, justice, peace, tenderness. That we remember how to imagine ourselves into the shoes of the stranger, and feel the texture of their life.

You may not see the road your work builds. It may be on the other side of the world, or you may not live to see it. But someone else will walk it. Then ten people will walk it. Then a city. Then maybe a whole country will wake up one morning and realize it has crossed a bridge it did not know you were building all along.

That is how you scale transformation. With narrative highways others may follow when they are ready.

You are here now. Needed now. To do the work.

That is quite a burden. How do you carry it?

6

EMOTIONAL SAFETY

The way we stay sane and whole as creative people is to accept a bifurcation of our lives. What I'm about to say may feel shocking. Yet it is the essential realization to ensure your emotional safety.

You are not your work.

Your work is a part of you, only a small part, and at a moment in time. When, in due course, your work makes it to the public sphere, the part of you that made it is already completed and you will have moved on.

This realization—that you are not your work—will give you emotional safety because, inevitably, some people won't like what you made. Or maybe a lot of people. That's okay, it doesn't matter. People have different needs and tastes at different times.

One evening, when I was the dramaturg at the Los Angeles Theatre Center, I came into the dressing room to wish the actors a good show that night. We had just opened a new piece by the visionary artist Reza Abdoh, and it was like nothing Los Angeles audiences had seen before, a collage of vulnerable and violent, costumed and naked, sensual and sacred. Some audience members walked out while others immediately bought tickets to see it a second time.

We'd built the dressing rooms as common areas, without individual "star" partitions, to encourage the equal collaborative nature of the theater. All the actors were together that night, in somber mood. There had been a terrible review in a major publication, more than terrible, vindictive, going after the director and the cast with personal attacks. Everyone had read the review, and its nastiness was blocking the energy they needed for the night's performance.

We had a long talk, did theater games, changed the energy and the show went on. We also learned a lesson: Don't read the reviews. They really don't matter for the work at hand.

This ability not to care what other people think has to be tempered with the capacity to listen, to hear our audience with big ears, to feel sensitively if our work is hitting the mark we intend. That can be difficult, because everyone will have an opinion!

But not all opinions matter. As a creative person, you will need to decide which opinions you will care about, and which ones you will disregard. Don't make this decision lightly, or do it based on economic concerns—such as, "If I get the right influencer on my side I'll sell a million tickets." In the first place, unless you truly value the reviewer's aesthetic, what they have to say won't be relevant for your work. And, in the second place, the number of tickets you sell will depend on a number of factors, many of which are very much in your capacity, which you'll discover later when you learn the 10 ten laws of culturenomics.

At the same time, don't choose opinions that will go easy on your work. The toughest input can be the most loving. There will be a few people who will take the time to experience your early drafts and give you useful feedback. Embrace them. Because our first drafts are rarely as good as we think they are.

How can I know which opinions count?

Here is an exercise for figuring out who to listen to: Take a sticky note, a small one, one that's an inch by an inch-and-a-half. Write the names of the people whose opinions matter to you. If they don't fit on the sticky note, they are not in your inner circle, and you can disregard them.

Determining who to listen to, and who not to listen to, is a key component of your emotional safety. You need feedback and input along the way, so you can shape and refine your work, but not so much that it will be damaging or stifle your progress.

You also need to fabricate a resilient outer layer. Thick and dense as a tortoise shell. Even if you don't feel you have this shell, even if it feels impossible to construct it because you are easily hurt and vulnerable, you can mentally pretend that it is there and, over time, it actually will grow. Because no matter how much you try to insulate yourself, some unconstructive voices will slip through, and you will have to find a way to keep them from penetrating too deeply.

Here's where the separation of self and work is invaluable. Even if negative people attack you, or you feel attacked by them, you can mentally disassemble that reaction to reaffirm that you are not your work, that their reaction is theirs not yours, and it is certainly not the reaction of people whose feedback truly matters to you.

Some creatives take this a step further, and create alternate personas through which they express themselves—and to protect themselves against rejection's razorblades. Janelle Monáe performed as Cindi Mayweather, an android living in a dystopian future. French surrealist Marcel Duchamp became Rrose Sélavy, who made and signed her own artworks. David Johansen, the original frontman for the New York Dolls, reinvented himself as lounge lizard Buster Poindexter so he would move into new forms of music.

Whatever path you take, however visibly you choose to identify with your creative acts, the separation between you and what you do is valid and healthy. All reactions, those that cheer and those that sting, are reactions to your work, work that is from a completed moment in time. Your work is not you.

So choosing who to listen to will be risky. I'm not great with risk. That's why I do what I do instead of driving a race car or skydiving.

7

RISK

Life is risk. Therefore:

Creative Life is risk.

It's a risk you have to take, because that is who you are. If you could do anything else, you would be doing it.

You will not take every risk your Creative Life offers; you will have to assess each opportunity as it comes along. You will also come to understand that everything has risks—there are risks in suppressing yourself, in not pursuing your foremost passions, just as there are risks in pursuing them.

So how do I assess? Feels like so much guesswork.

Glad you asked. Because there actually is a way to do it. At first, or in unfamiliar situations, this will take some time. Later in your creative career, it will become intuitive. That's when people start saying, "You're a curmudgeon, you think everything won't work." Which is what people say to me a lot. But it's really just pattern recognition, having seen so many situations, so many deals, people, places, projects, variations, personalities, reactions, that one begins to get the sense of things early on. You'll develop pattern recognition, too.

Let's say you're starting a collaboration with a composer to write a song for a Disney musical. Here are some of the risks: You won't collaborate well, the song won't be good, Disney will reject it, the musical itself won't be good enough to open, Disney will go out of business.

Now, how real are these risks? It is highly unlikely that Disney will go out of business. But it is likely that the musical won't open, because most creative projects don't succeed. Will you and your collaborator work well together? That depends on how well you know each other, and if you have collaborated before.

Knowing how big each risk is will allow you to decide if you want to go forward. If you do go forward, if the risks feel workable for you, you can monitor them over time. You can seek to manage and mitigate them, and evaluate where you are at nodal points, to see if you should change or pivot, keep going or walk away.

Even with all of that, it's hard to tell which risks are worthwhile.

Well, as a creative person, you are more likely to say "yes" than "no" to opportunities, right?

Right. Because I can always imagine how great they would be.

True. That's a special talent creative people have. But your capacity to understand risk will allow you, over time, to make better assessments. Time is the only resource that is truly limited, and you will learn to guard your creative time wisely and well. As you move along, "yes" will be more infrequent and more meaningful; and you will find that "no, this isn't right for me right now," will become an easier line of dialogue.

Many of the choices you make, indeed, most of them, won't bear the fruit you first envisioned. But that doesn't mean they were a waste of time. You will find that one experience leads to another, that along the way you find collaborators who are truer and more meaningful, who become frequent companions on the route.

Your capacity to assess risk and embrace the right risks enables a sustainable life.

What do you mean by "sustainable"? Are you talking about finances?

8

SUSTAINING

If you expend all your creative risk-tolerance in sporadic volcanic bursts, you won't last long. You need to go the distance.

Sustainability goes hand in hand with preparation. We have all heard stories of great artistic work being crafted in days or hours. Perhaps that's when the work emerged from fingers or brush. But the artist had been working internally, preparing persistently, for years. I wrote the bulk of my first book in one blazing forty-eight-hour weekend. But I had been working on it, subterranean, for decades.

When we talk about a sustainable life, most people think about having enough money to keep going. That's important, but it's not the most important.

To sustain us, the most essential element is relationships.

The people in your life have a great deal to do with your mood, capacity, and drive. If they accept you and your art, you will find it easier to do your work. If they don't, you will battle their negative reactions at the same time as trying to do your work—which is battle enough.

I've had both situations in my life. When I had close relationships with people who didn't like my creative life, were not prepared to ride the roller coaster of it, and disparaged my aesthetic choices, I found I was unproductive. When I am surrounded by people who accept my life, or, even better, encourage it, my work flows more freely.

I'm glad you've had sustaining relationships, and I hope you always do, but I don't have that now.

I understand. There is more than one kind of relationship that sustains us. The good news is that you only need a single core relationship to sustain you. If it isn't your family or primary romantic relationship, it may be a mentor. It may be a creative circle, like a writer's group, that gets together regularly. It may be a teacher who offers a supportive hand. It may mean locating yourself within a community of creative humans, so your passion and drive are valued.

I have my marriage, my family, my creative communities. They get me through, sometimes just because I know they are there. Without at least one sustaining relationship, you will still persist, because you must, but the path will be more painful.

A key to any healthy relationship is that it must be reciprocal. You cannot only take. Seek and build your key relationships before you need them; support and sustain others, putting your good energy into the bank, so it may be dedicated to you when the time comes.

There are other ways to sustain, too.

Your body is the instrument of your expression. Attend to your health and physical well-being. Many great artists have led outwardly boring lives to accomplish this: They work at the same time every day, exercise at the same time, eat at the same time—sometimes even the same meal every day. Toni Morrison awoke daily before sunup, and before her family awoke, so she could write in morning quiet. Author and journalist Robert Caro puts on a suit and tie every day he writes so he feels like he is "at work." Haruki Murakami writes from 4:00 a.m. to 9:00 a.m., runs or swims in the afternoon, barely socializes, is in bed by 9:00 p.m. With this level of discipline, these artists sustained themselves by prioritizing their creative work over the siren songs that others find alluring.

Exercise, food, schedule, rest—along with relationships, these are hallmarks of your commitment to sustaining your creative life. You may appear boring to the outside world; inside, you will be fire. These practices of personal sustainability will give you the resolved certitude to leap and the confidence to land.

But what if I don't have anywhere to do my work at the moment?

9

WORKING ENVIRONMENT

Your creative environment is your private collaborator—visible and knowable only to you, unless you allow others into your sanctum.

And it is a sanctum—a sacred place where you do the ritual of your work.

Today, I am writing this in a loft in the Arts District in downtown Los Angeles. It is my personal studio space. I could choose to work at home; instead I choose to get up and drive to my "office" at 6:00 a.m. Monday through Friday. It's a converted brick warehouse building built in 1907 and my loft has a twelve-foot ceiling and large windows. It is expansive and has no interior walls so I feel openness and possibility. I move around unimpeded.

I have had the luxury of developing this space over time to meet my creative needs. But even before I had this space, I always had *a* space. For years I stationed myself at a back table at Groundworks Coffee. Other years, as my kids were growing up, I faced my desk to the wall and mentally evaporated the stuff of life behind me.

Mystery writer Harlan Coben likes to write on airplanes. He has to stay in his seat and doesn't have distractions. Virgil Abloh, who founded fashion brand Off-White and was the artistic director for Louis Vuitton menswear, worked in public spaces because seeing people in their cultural action inspired him. Iconic, revolutionary architect Le Corbusier, who designed monumental public edifices, worked out his visions in a tiny, remote mountain cabin. Maya Angelou went to hotel rooms to write; upon checking in she removed all decorations: Only the Bible remained, and she brought with her a dictionary and a bottle of sherry.

You need your space, too, whatever and wherever it is. It's the regular ritual of going there that matters.

When you have your space, treat it well. Remove clutter, because a messy visual field can distract your thoughts. (Unless, of course, you thrive in clutter. Some people do!) When you arrive, set yourself up. When you are done, make a ritual of closing the space, reorganizing it, so it will be ready for you the next day.

If I'm on a budget…?

Use what you have and where you have. Rearrange the furniture. Put up a vision board or something else that will inspire you as you stare ahead trying to figure out what to do next. If you are in a place you control, get good lighting—try tungsten-balanced LEDs or light bulbs, as they are easier on your eyes and psyche. Control your audio environment, too—you may like quiet or sound, music or fuzz noise, and if your creative space is a public space, pull on your headphones and transport into your own world.

Okay. I get it. Still, all that control sounds a bit boring.

10

CURIOSITY

If you're not curious about what comes next, perhaps you should ask yourself why.

Curiosity is the engine that powers long creative careers, audience engagement, and the unique relevance of your work. Just as your environment is your private collaborator, curiosity is your internal co-conspirator.

You can discern this by looking at creatives who have had long careers. They continually reinvent themselves to the point where their later-in-life work can feel fresher than their early work. The best film directors with long careers—Agnès Varda, Akira Kurosawa, Steven Spielberg, Ridley Scott, Martin Scorsese, Clint Eastwood—make films into their seventies, eighties, and beyond, with the passion of youth because they are continuously curious, curious about technologies, style, narrative choices. Brilliant cellist Yo-Yo Ma's curiosity has driven him to explore much of the world: He has collaborated with musicians from China, India, Turkey, Iran, Appalachia, Japan, West Africa, and Central Asia, in styles as diverse as jazz, tango, and experimental minimalism. Joe Rogan owes his massive popularity to his insatiable curiosity: His accessible style is always exploring, questioning, seeking answers.

Curiosity of the artist drives curiosity of the audience, and that's crucial to sales, downloads, and word-of-mouth. Curiosity is the reason click-bait works, why Google became a $2 trillion company, and why people binge-watch: We want to know more.

Most importantly, for you as a creative, your curiosity will take your work out of what's normal and expected. By which I mean, your curiosity will keep your work from being boring. You can't innovate or break new ground until questions drive you.

Sometimes I cannot feel curious about anything. Whatever I have to say has been said before, whatever I might make has been made before. I feel inanimate, a part of the scenery.

Make a different choice.

Dive deep into something, anything. Free resources for learning abound, and learning is infinite. Science reveals that learning and questioning activate the brain's reward system, meaning that the more you do it the more you want to do it.

Theodore Sturgeon, a science-fiction writer, was approaching the end of his long career as I was growing up. I met him at a writing convention when I was a teenager. He wore a silver lapel pin: the letter Q with an arrow running through it. "What's that?" I asked. "I had it made," he said. "It means, Ask the next question."

To provoke your curiosity, do just that. Ask the next question of others, of yourself. What's next? What if? Why not? Could we? Could I?

Here's my next question: Which way should I go?

11

FUNCTIONAL OR AESTHETIC?

A piece of plywood, two-by-fours, some nails: a functional table.

Sand it and lacquer it, add the emblem of a lotus: an aesthetic table.

You and I can have dinner at either table.

Every creative work exists on a spectrum between pure function and pure aesthetics. Is your design solving a problem, or is it meant to conjure a profound reaction?

Do I have to make that distinction, or can it be some of both?

Sometimes it can do both. Making an intentional decision about where your work will land on this spectrum will shape how you approach it. When you start something, take a moment to consider: What is its primary purpose?

Well, I want my work to work. But I also want it to be beautiful.

Aesthetic is not panacea. Mies van der Rohe's Barcelona chair is a classic of aesthetic design. It was unveiled in 1929 in the German Pavilion of the Barcelona Exposition, groundbreaking in its use of materials and structure, Bauhaus-iconic and oft-copied today. I find it uncomfortable to sit in; the recline angle hurts your back so much it motivates you to get up and walk around.

Functional is not panacea either. So much entertainment media made by what I call the Entertainment Industrial Complex, that is, by streaming services and movie studios, feels purely functional—designed for easy audience gratification, which, for the distributors offering these "content products," means subscriber retention and ticket sales. These movies and series are forgettable and evaporate from the mind before the credits roll, if you even get that far.

Jony Ive's designs for Apple are one of the best marriages of aesthetics and function, and now practically everybody's got one in their hands. Ive worked collaboratively with Apple's engineers to make sure they would function well and applied his visual and tactile sensibility. There are no straight lines in nature, he observed; the rounded corners of Apple products broke away from the rectilinear past and made them feel instantly comfortable.

Or take a look at Coco Chanel's designs. They are straightforward, elegant, supremely functional—and she turned functionality into her aesthetic.

The best way to think about creative work that *works* is that it has integrity. If it seeks to solve a problem, to be functional, it *functions.* If it seeks beauty, it is *radiant.*

Decide what you're going for, who your audience is, how they will best experience your work—then create with integrity toward its purpose.

I want to be creative! It's just that life keeps getting in the way—you know, work, responsibilities, distractions.

12

SHOW UP FOR WORK (TIME MANAGEMENT)

Your creative life is your job. Like any profession, it requires commitment, discipline, and structure. The romantic myth of the free-spirited artist, waiting for inspiration to strike, doesn't hold up in the real world. Creativity flourishes when paired with professionalism—and professionalism begins with showing up for work every day.

If you wait for inspiration, you'll wait forever. Creativity isn't about waiting—it's about showing up, sitting down, stapling your butt to the chair, doing the work. You wouldn't tell a boss, "I'll start working when I feel inspired." You show up, and in doing so, you create the conditions where inspiration can find you.

Establishing a routine is one of the most powerful ways to take control of your creative practice. Designate specific hours—even if it's just thirty minutes a day—where you commit to your work. No excuses. The mind thrives on consistency. If mornings are when you're most clear-headed, make that your sacred creative time. If nights are quieter, set that time aside. The goal is to build a habit, to create a rhythm where your mind learns that *this* is the time to create.

What if I sit down and nothing comes?

That's where structure helps. Before each session, set an intention. What do you want to accomplish? A sentence? A rough draft? A melody? A sketch? Even if you don't finish, having a clear goal keeps you moving forward. Break big projects into smaller tasks. Progress, not perfection.

By being intentional with your time, you can balance creative work with other responsibilities. Consider time-blocking—carving out specific periods for different tasks so that your creative work doesn't get squeezed out. If you have a day job, your creative time might be early morning or late evening. The key is commitment.

Sometimes, I'm just exhausted.

That's fair. You don't need to burn yourself out. But preparation helps. If you set up your workspace the night before, if you jot down notes or sketch ideas in free moments, you'll enter your creative time ready to dive in rather than wasting it warming up.

Taylor Swift is one of the most disciplined creatives out there. (Yes, I'm a Swiftie.) She started training for her Eras tour six months in advance; her routine included running on a treadmill every day while singing the entire Eras setlist aloud.

Structure doesn't kill creativity. It protects it.

In addition to structure, creativity needs space. Life happens. Inspiration might strike at unexpected moments. The key is knowing the difference between genuine creative spontaneity and just making excuses. A routine gives you discipline, but adaptability lets you adjust without losing momentum.

Professionalism isn't about getting paid—it's about how seriously you take yourself. Meeting your own deadlines, being punctual for creative collaborations, setting expectations, communicating clearly. When you show up for your creative work as if it matters, other people will start to believe it matters, too.

Procrastination and perfectionism are the biggest obstacles creatives face. Not every session will produce gold. Some days will feel like failures. That's okay. Keep showing up. Limit distractions—turn off notifications, find a quiet space. And don't do it alone. Join a community, find an accountability partner, share your progress.

Showing up every day sounds good in theory, but does it really work?

Yes. Because showing up isn't just about discipline—it's about respect. Respect for your craft, your dreams, and yourself. Treat your creative life like the extraordinary job it is, and it will reward you with clarity, growth, and fulfillment.

What if I don't know what I'm doing yet?

13

YOU DON'T HAVE TO KNOW WHERE YOU ARE GOING

When you begin, it's like stepping into a dense fog, the kind that blurs everything more than a few steps ahead. You don't know if you're about to stumble onto a welcoming meadow or trip over a tree root. And yet, you step forward anyway. You move because something inside you whispers that you have to, even if you're not sure why.

I feel like I need a plan. A direction, an outline. Some sense of what I'm doing before I even start.

That's what the world teaches us, isn't it? Map it out, plot the points, calculate the return-on-investment. But creativity doesn't work like that. It can't. If it did, David Bowie might never have made *Low*.

Time-travel with me to Berlin in the 1970s. Bowie had fled Los Angeles, a place that had swallowed him whole. He was fragmented, uncertain, creatively spent. Berlin was his escape hatch, the raw and gritty city a reflection of the fractured man he'd become. When he stepped into the studio with Brian Eno, there was no grand vision for the album that would eventually emerge. They didn't even have songs, just shards of ideas—some half-formed melodies, snips of sound, willingness to experiment.

Put yourself there: Bowie at the piano, fingering a haunting riff that sounded like a dream. Eno, always the provocateur, pulling out his deck of "Oblique Strategies" cards—prompts designed to disrupt conventional thinking. "Try something you've never done before," one card might say. Or, "Abandon normal instruments." It was chaos. Inspiring chaos. They followed threads of inspiration wherever they led, not knowing what they'd find at the end. The result? An album that redefined not only Bowie's career but the entire trajectory of modern music.

Here's what Bowie understood, and you may begin to understand, too: You don't have to know where you're going. In fact, not knowing is the point. Uncertainty isn't the enemy of creativity; it's its greatest ally. The moments when you feel most lost are often the moments when something extraordinary is quietly waiting to be discovered.

That's terrifying.

Trust that the process, as messy and unpredictable as it is, will eventually lead you somewhere worthwhile.

This isn't about blind faith. It's about understanding that the act of moving forward—of writing that first awkward sentence, sketching that imperfect line, recording that dissonant chord—is what allows the map to reveal itself. You don't find the path before you walk it. You find it by walking.

Yes, sometimes you'll stumble. You'll fall flat on your face, and it will hurt. You'll wonder if it's all worth it, if you should have taken a safer, more predictable road. That's normal. It's human. Every creative person I've ever met—no matter how successful—has felt that way. But here's the thing: You'll get up. You'll keep going. Because deep down, you know that this isn't just what you do. It's who you are.

As we move forward, hold on to this thought: The uncertainty you feel isn't a sign of failure. It's a sign that you're on the right track. And if you ever feel overwhelmed by the ambiguity, remember that the detours—the unexpected twists and turns—often lead to the fertile destinations.

Now, let me ask you something. How do you feel when you approach your work? Excited? Hesitant?

Maybe a little of both. Which one is right?

14

AMBIVALENCE

Creativity is messy.

It pulls you into the parts of yourself that don't have neat, easy answers. You're in love with your work, it's going to change the world! You're drowning in doubt, it's crap! That push and pull—that ambivalence—isn't a flaw.

It's exhausting.

It's a sign you care.

That's the creative process. Mihaly Csikszentmihalyi, one of the leading researchers on creativity, the psychologist who named the "flow" state, observed that artists and innovators live in tension. You're drawn to your work because it speaks to something profound within you, but it's also maddeningly elusive. The gap between what you imagine and what you can create feels impossible to bridge.

So, what do I do with all this doubt?

You don't have a choice but to work with it. Leonard Cohen spent seven years writing "Hallelujah," filling notebooks with lyrics, discarding and rewriting verses over and over. He loved the song, and he also doubted it, struggled with it. At one point, there were 180 verses. He nearly abandoned it. That ambivalence pushed him deeper. It's what made the song a masterpiece.

Sometimes, the weight of it makes me want to quit.

The tension can be exhausting. When the weight of self-doubt gets too heavy, escape routes appear. Drugs, alcohol, sex, overwork. Maybe they'll distract us, spike us with a burst of pleasure, quiet the noise inside. Maybe they'll dissolve the fear that maybe we're not good enough. The terror that this time, we'll fail.

It makes me feel broken.

You're not broken. You're human. Creative people carry our work like a second skin. Or our first skin. We don't just make things; we pour ourselves into them. And when that weight becomes too much, we reach for whatever numbs the fear.

But those things don't actually help. They feel like relief in the moment, but they take more than they give. Drugs and alcohol cloud judgment and rob clarity. Casual distractions mask the loneliness but don't fill the void. Overwork feels like progress, but it's just running from our own minds. These behaviors aren't the problem. They're symptoms. Signs of deeper fears: fear of failure, fear of being seen, fear of never being enough.

That's hard. How do we even talk about it?

We're talking now. Keep reading. Or talk to someone else: a friend, a mentor, a therapist. Let them remind you that you're not alone, that your worth isn't tied to your work, that your struggles don't define you. Seeking help isn't weakness; it's strength.

Impostor syndrome is another voice that creeps in. That voice is a liar. It tells you that you don't belong, that you're not as talented as people think. But here's the truth. Doubt doesn't mean you're failing. It means you're growing.

I don't know if I'll ever stop doubting myself.

You are not an impostor. You are someone brave enough to create something out of nothing.

Every great creative has faced this. Greta Gerwig, while directing *Lady Bird*, rode an emotional roller coaster. Some days, she was sure the film was the best thing she'd ever done. Other days, she was convinced it was a disaster. That ambivalence pushed her to refine, to deepen, to make every scene better. In the end, the very feelings that made her doubt the work were the ones that made it great. She once said that you can never fully grasp art, "that's why it's satisfyingly unsatisfying forever."

My ambivalence is the greatest creative obstacle.

Love your work enough to stay with it and doubt it enough to make it better. In this pressure-cooker, profound vision happens: It's the prequel to any great work, when your work starts to take shape in a way only you can see.

Your vision is your most intimate sight; you alone can open your eye to it.

Vision with purpose is what sets the extraordinary apart from the ordinary.

Most of us are just trying to get through the day. How do I even begin to know the purpose?

15

UNKNOWN KNOWNS: SIGHT PAST THE HORIZON

Great leaders and great creatives share a unique capacity: the ability to see past the horizon. To envision what doesn't yet exist but could. To peer into the multiple fogs of possibility and bring back something clear, compelling, undeniable.

Look beyond what's immediately in front of you. Deadlines, projects, to-do lists—these things keep your focus narrow. Visionaries don't just see what's directly ahead. They anticipate what's coming, what's possible, what's needed. And then they make it real, so real that others can't help but follow.

That sounds like a gift, not something you can learn.

It's a skill—one you can cultivate. It starts with asking questions no one else is asking. Or saying the truth no one else is speaking. What's missing? What are people longing for, even if they don't know it yet? What does the world need that it doesn't yet have? These aren't easy questions, and the answers aren't always obvious. But the act of asking them shifts your perspective from the present to the possible.

Let's go back to Virgil Abloh. When he founded his brand Off-White, blending streetwear with high fashion, the concept was dismissed by traditionalists as a gimmick. To them, streetwear was casual, ephemeral, unworthy of the haute couture world. But Abloh saw something they didn't. He understood that younger generations were hungry for a new kind of cultural expression—something that honored their roots while breaking the boundaries of what fashion could be. He didn't just dream it; he saw it, articulated it, and made it happen. The result? A global movement that reshaped the fashion industry and made him a creative icon.

That makes sense, but what if people don't get it?

Vision requires resilience. It demands the courage to face doubt—your own and others'—and keep going anyway. But vision only takes you so far. You have to believe in it so deeply that you're willing to risk failure, ridicule, and rejection to bring it to life. That belief becomes your anchor, the thing that keeps you steady when waves of uncertainty threaten to knock you down.

But having a great idea isn't enough, is it?

You may see the future with perfect clarity, but if you can't communicate it, it will remain just that—a vision. You must find a way to express your idea so vividly that others can see it, too. This is where Artist becomes Leader.

So how do I develop my vision?

Begin with curiosity. Look for the gaps, notice what's missing, imagine what could fill the void. Then, take the time to articulate your vision. Don't be afraid to start with an ugly first draft—most great ideas begin as fragments. Refine them, test them, share them with people you trust. Listen to their feedback, but don't let their doubts eclipse your belief.

What if I'm wrong?

You might be. That's part of the process. Seeing past the horizon is a deeply personal act of faith. It requires trusting your perspective, even when others can't yet see what you see. But when you persist—when you hold on to your vision and are able to bring it into being—you will give the world something it didn't know it needed.

How can I shape the intangible into something tangible? How can I transform the invisible into something everyone can see? How do I do that?

16

BUILD YOUR INSIDE STRENGTHS

Start on the inside. Of you.

Creativity isn't just about the brilliance of your ideas or the elegance of your execution. It's about endurance. It's about having the inner strength to keep going when the world doesn't understand you or when your work feels like broken shards you cannot put back together. To walk the creative path, you need a solid foundation—emotional resilience, mental focus, physical vitality. These are the muscles that carry you through the moments when inspiration falters and the work feels like an uphill climb.

It's easy to get stuck in self-doubt. One bad day, and it feels like I'll never get anywhere.

That's why emotional strength matters. We romanticize creativity as something spontaneous and magical, but the truth is, a lot if it is a grind. Emotional resilience helps you navigate the inevitable storms of self-doubt, rejection, setbacks. It's what keeps you rooted when your work faces criticism or when the voice in your head whispers that you'll never measure up. (By the way, don't believe that voice—it isn't yours.) Resilience isn't about being unshakable; it's about being able to recover, to bounce back. It's about moving past the limitations of your brain to the limitlessness of your mind. If I have one strength as a producer, probably my primary strength, it's that people can say "no" to me one hundred times and I will keep going. Knock me down; I'm getting back up.

Dr. Brené Brown (have you read *Daring Greatly?*) writes about resilience as the ability to embrace vulnerability—to show up, be seen, and take risks despite the fear of failure. Vulnerability isn't weakness; it's a survival skill. It is necessary. It opens you to feedback, growth, and connection, all of which are essential to your creative work. Emotional strength doesn't mean you won't feel pain or disappointment; it means those feelings won't stop you. This is the key point of Dr. Brown's exceptional work.

But sometimes, I just can't focus. My mind jumps from one thing to another, and I can't get into the flow.

Creativity also demands focus. In a world swarming with distractions, cultivating mental clarity is more important than ever. When you train your mind to stay present, you can enter a state of flow, where time disappears and your ideas accelerate with an energy of their own.

Ava DuVernay credits much of her success to her ability to cultivate internal strength. Her mornings start with mindfulness practices that ground her for the day ahead. She works in focused blocks, managing the enormous demands of her creative projects with precision and care. As a Black woman navigating an industry that often fails to make space for voices like hers, DuVernay has spoken openly about the importance of resilience and self-discipline. Her success didn't come from waiting for inspiration to strike; it came from building the strength to meet her creative challenges head-on.

That makes sense, but what about the physical part? I don't think about my body when I'm making my art.

That's a mistake many creatives make. It's hard to do your best work when your body is depleted. Your physical form is the medium through which your spiritual self emanates. Regular exercise doesn't just boost your physical health—it sharpens your mind and stabilizes your emotions. The body fuels the brain, and the brain fuels your creativity. Building habits that nurture your physical health—whether it's a morning walk, yoga, or simply getting enough sleep—creates the stamina you need to sustain your creative work over the long haul.

So where do I start?

"Know thyself": Philosophers have been saying that for two thousand years. Take an honest inventory of your emotional, mental, and physical health. What areas need attention? Where are you struggling? Then, commit to small, consistent changes. Build habits that strengthen you from the inside out, and don't underestimate the power of rest, reflection, and care. Creativity is about how you live as much as what you make.

As you strengthen your inner foundation, you'll find that you're better equipped to face the challenges of the creative path. You'll have the resilience to bounce back from failures, the focus to stay in the flow, and the energy to see your projects through. These are your lifelines. They carry you when inspiration wanes, when the work gets hard, and when doubt creeps in.

And as you cultivate these strengths, something remarkable will happen: You will support more than your work. You will support yourself. Your creativity isn't a separate part of you—it's woven into every aspect of who you are. Supporting your personal strengths becomes a way of nurturing your creative spirit.

Feels like I need to cultivate a whole ecosystem inside myself before the real creative work can come outside myself. How do I do that?

17

SUPPORT YOUR INSIDE STRENGTHS

In the fall of 490 BC, the Athenians, heavily outnumbered, defeated the invading Persian army on the plains of Marathon. Pheidippides, a professional runner in the Athenian army, sprinted to Athens to share the good news. His long run inspired the present-day marathon race. Likewise, creativity is a marathon, but I want us all to have a better outcome: Pheidippides announced, "We have won!" as he entered the Athenian Senate, then dropped dead. So goes the legend.

For the legend we are writing for ourselves right now: We need to keep going.

To sustain the long, circuitous journey, you must learn to support the strengths you've built inside yourself. These strengths—emotional resilience, mental clarity, physical vitality—are not luxuries. They're necessities. They're the bedrock that keeps you steady when the world around you shakes and when the work feels like too much.

I thought passion and hard work would be enough.

That's what I believed, too. Worse, perhaps, I believed that if I worked longer and harder than anyone else, I would be rewarded. Early in my career at Disney, when Disney was a small studio struggling to make a comeback, the work ethic was, "If you don't come in on

Saturday, don't bother to come in on Sunday." I followed that, but I was newly married, and soon there would be a baby on the way. I remember being in my office, night outside, staring at a script that I was supposed to write notes on for the next morning, and realizing I couldn't do it and still be a person worthy of having a response. I packed it in, went home, cancelled the next day's meeting, told my boss it was better to wait until we were ready than to do a poor job. Over the years I spent at the studio, I developed a practice of working on half the development projects as my peers, but I got more of them green-lit into movies. If I wanted to create work that mattered, I had to take care of the person creating it.

What does that actually look like?

It starts with radical prioritization. I gave every time-based decision the five-year test: What would I remember in five years: Staying late? Or going home and having dinner with the kids? Most nights, the kids won. And that gave me resilience.

Creative work is full of highs and lows—moments of triumph and moments of rejection. Resilience means you will feel the sting of a setback and you will recover from it. One of the most powerful tools I've found for this is reframing. When something goes wrong—a failed pitch, a rejected idea, a scathing critique—ask yourself: What can I learn from this? How can this challenge make me better? Because creative life is a life of people saying "no."

Over time, I started to see patterns. The setbacks that once felt devastating became opportunities. Emotional triggers, like fear of failure or the need for validation, became easier to recognize—and to manage. I learned to use my emotions to my advantage. I learned to hear "no" as "not right now."

But what if I just can't focus?

The creative mind is a wild horse—full of energy but it needs direction. Without focus, you can feel scattered and unproductive. This is where mindfulness comes in. Whether it's a daily meditation practice, a morning journaling session, or simply taking five minutes to breathe deeply and clear your head, mindfulness creates the mental space you need to do your best work.

When I first started practicing yoga, I didn't know the effect it would have. Moving through postures and focusing on my breath felt counterproductive when I had so much to do. It was hard to quiet my monkey-mind. But I committed to it, and discovered that yoga is not really a physical practice—it is about the breath, only the breath, the evenness and effortlessness of the breath; its physical positions are there to remind you to allow unaltered breathing even under stress. Over time, I perceived a shift. I learned to breathe through my work, not just down-dog. My thoughts became less cluttered, my decisions sharper. The moments of overwhelm that once derailed me became easier to navigate; my mind became more flexible as my body did.

And the physical part? Does it really make that much of a difference?

It does. I see physical health as nonnegotiable. Regular exercise isn't just about staying fit; it's about feeding your brain the oxygen and energy it needs to think clearly and creatively. My best ideas come to me during downtime, when I turn away from daily chaos, maybe when I'm walking, when the rhythm of my steps and the fresh air quiet the noise in my head. And I value sleep. Don't underestimate the power of a good night's rest. Creativity doesn't thrive on exhaustion; it thrives on renewal.

It sounds great, but life gets in the way. There's always something demanding my time.

Boundaries matter. As creatives, we often feel the pressure to say yes to every opportunity, every request, every collaboration. But your time and energy are finite. Protecting them isn't selfish—it's essential.

One of the most transformative exercises I have is a "boundaries manifesto." I list the things I need to protect my creative energy: uninterrupted time to work, space for rest and recovery, the ability to decline commitments that don't align with my goals. Putting it in writing is empowering. It becomes a guidepost, reminding me that every "no" I say is really a "yes" to my work, my health, and my vision.

And if I do all of this—support my strengths, set my boundaries—will it get easier?

The creative journey is long, and the road isn't always smooth. But when you support your inside strengths—emotionally, mentally, and physically—you build a resilient foundation. Your creativity deserves that kind of care. And so do you.

But there's one more piece to this puzzle. As much as you build your strengths and set your boundaries, there will come moments when you have to step into the unknown.

Sounds scary. How do you suggest I step into that unknown?

18

TRUST YOUR INSTINCTS

When the map doesn't show the way, you have only your instincts to guide you.

Instincts are the compass of your work, a tool you carry even when the terrain is unfamiliar. Instincts may feel unsteady, especially at the outset, like a flickering light in the fog. Yet they will be your best guide through uncharted territory. Trusting them is an act of courage—and a practice that grows stronger with time. Every creative journey begins here, with a gut feeling that says, "This is worth exploring."

Playwright Ellen McLaughlin felt her instincts pull toward the ancient Greek dramas. It made no sense—she didn't read Greek. But she followed the urge. Her theatrical adaptations of those plays became preeminent and have been performed worldwide.

I don't know if I can trust my instincts yet. What if they lead me the wrong way?

When you're just starting out, trusting your instincts can feel reckless, even naïve. They might be unrefined, misaligned, or occasionally wrong.

Actually, here's the truth. When you are starting out, your instincts will be terrible. There's no getting around that, no shortcut. But they are the raw material for your creative decision-making. They're shaped by your experiences, your observations, your unique way of seeing the world. Follow them, even when they seem to lead in an unexpected or risky direction. That's how they begin to sharpen.

Shonda Rhimes understands this better than most. Early in her career, the television industry had a rigid playbook: Shows looked a certain way, characters fit specific molds, and stories rarely ventured outside a narrow band of convention. But Rhimes trusted her gut, even when it told her to go against the grain. She wrote bold characters that didn't just fit into the world of television—they expanded it. Shows like *Grey's Anatomy* and *Scandal* were groundbreaking. Rhimes took a leap of faith on her instincts, and they carried her into territory no one else could see. She created new territory.

Sometimes I second-guess myself. How do I know if it's instinct or just fear?

Instincts aren't always comfortable. They often come wrapped in doubt, and the louder the stakes, the more doubt they bring. Even seasoned creatives experience this. Trusting your instincts doesn't mean banishing uncertainty. It means acting despite it, recognizing that doubt is part of the process. I like Steven Pressfield's book, *The War of Art.* (Have you read it?) He describes doubt as resistance—a force that rises in proportion to the importance of your work.

Resistance doesn't mean your instincts are wrong. It means you're onto something. When you encounter it, you're also ready to hold the emotional strength to feel pain and disappointment while not letting that pain stop you—accepting and protecting your vulnerability, because that's what makes your art possible, while also moving forward.

Have you ever made a choice that felt completely irrational at the time, but later you realized it was exactly right?

One of the first films I worked on had a unique title. An off-putting title. The movie was terrific, preview audiences responded well to it, but the title seemed completely at odds with commercial success. The head of distribution set a meeting with those of us in the creative group. "We have to change the title," he demanded. "All of it. Listen to those words. 'Dead.' Nobody wants to go to a movie about death. Then, 'Poets.' Do you only want poetry teachers to buy tickets? And, 'Society.' You've got to be kidding. It's elitist. It's terrible. We can't open the movie unless you change the title."

We didn't change the title. We followed our instincts. Even to this day, everywhere I go in the world, someone has seen *Dead Poets Society* and shares that it made an indelible mark on their lives. Sometimes your instincts lead you to the edge of the map because that's where the treasure is.

Feedback can be a tricky companion to instincts. It's essential, but it can also drown out your inner voice if you let it. The goal isn't to shut out feedback but to filter it. Ask yourself, "Does this resonate with me?" If the answer is no, trust that. If the answer is yes, let that resonance refine your instincts rather than replace them. The balance between external input and internal guidance is where you'll find your voice.

Will my instincts ever be perfect?

Perfection doesn't exist. But your instincts will always be uniquely yours. They're a reflection of who you are, what you've seen, and what you bring to the world. Trust them enough to start, and trust the process to sharpen them. Over time, your instincts will become your greatest creative strength.

As you build this trust, you'll start to notice something extraordinary. Your work will begin to improve.

So I'm not chasing perfection? Isn't that the point?

19

PLUS FOR EXCELLENCE

Excellence isn't a grand leap. It's the result of tiny, incremental, deliberate steps forward—a mindset of constantly asking, "How can this be even better?" At Pixar, they call this "plussing." It's a philosophy that has shaped some of the most memorable films ever made. With every tweak and improvement, every extra bit of effort, something good transforms into something extraordinary.

The idea of plussing isn't about perfection. It's about growth. It's about taking what you have, whether it's a draft, a design, or a melody, and finding ways to elevate it without losing its essence. In other words, when you're plussing you only give critique to improve, not to denigrate. Excellence, after all, isn't a destination. It's a mindset. It's about committing to the process of improvement, no matter how small the steps may seem.

At Pixar, this philosophy permeates everything they do. During the production of *Toy Story 2*, the team wasn't satisfied with "good enough." They reworked and reanimated entire sequences, even when it meant starting from scratch. One scene in particular, that poignant moment when Jessie's backstory is revealed, was plussed over and over again until it captured exactly the right mix of emotion and storytelling. The result was a film that exceeded expectations, cementing its place as a classic.

That sounds exhausting.

Plussing is an iterative process. As Ed Catmull describes in *Creativity, Inc.* (another good book you might enjoy), this culture of collaboration and incremental enhancements is what makes Pixar's work stand out. It does not come from naming, "here's what's wrong"; it's about finding opportunities to make something already good even better.

The beauty of plussing is that it breaks down the daunting task of excellence into manageable pieces. You identify small, specific ways to elevate your work. Targeted improvement. Whether you're writing, painting, coding, or composing, the principle is the same: Finish your first version, then ask, "What's one thing I can improve?" Don't get stuck waiting for inspiration or chasing an unattainable standard of perfection. Focus on small, steady improvements. Excellence is a habit.

Collaboration plays a vital role in the plussing process. When you invite trusted peers to review your work, you gain fresh perspectives that can spark ideas you hadn't considered. We'll talk more about collaboration later. For now, the key is to frame feedback as an opportunity for growth. Each refinement becomes a victory. As you build on these victories, you develop the habit of excellence—one small plus at a time.

I'm looking over some of my work now. There are weak places I can identify, and there are others I can sense need rethinking. What do I do about them?

20

MINUS THE MEDIOCRE

Like chiseling a marble block to reveal a statue, removing the mediocre allows your best work to shine through. Delete it.

Mediocrity dilutes excellence.

Keeping weak elements in your work lowers the overall quality, making it harder for your strongest ideas to stand out. Walter Isaacson, in his book *Steve Jobs*, describes how Jobs prioritized simplicity by cutting unnecessary features, leading to iconic product designs. Subtraction isn't destruction; it's refinement.

Editing feels like the opposite of creating.

Taking away what doesn't serve the work is just as important as adding new ideas. Twyla Tharp, in *The Creative Habit*, emphasizes editing as a crucial part of any artistic practice. The more precise you become about what stays and what goes, the stronger your work becomes.

Eliminating mediocrity creates focus. When you strip away what's not working, you free up mental and creative energy to concentrate on what truly matters. The cut, severe as it may seem at first, means that you feel that what you will make is better than what you have right now; it requires that you have faith in yourself as a *creative being*.

Which you are.

Then you sharpen what remains until it has undeniable impact.

Coco Chanel revolutionized fashion by rejecting the overdecorated, restrictive styles of her era. Her designs focused on simplicity, elegance, and functionality—eliminating anything unnecessary. This less-is-more philosophy made her work timeless. By removing the mediocre, Chanel didn't just redefine fashion; she created an enduring standard of excellence. "Simplicity is the keynote to all true elegance," she said.

How do I recognize what's mediocre?

Start by identifying what isn't working. Review your work and pinpoint the elements that feel weak, unnecessary, or out of place. Ask yourself, "Does this serve the overall vision?" At times, you might keep something that you know you'll cut or replace—like a dummy lyric—because it lets you move forward to see the whole: Later, you can go back and cut some more.

The process of cutting isn't about criticizing your work; it's about respecting it. It's about believing in its potential so deeply that you're willing to strip away anything that detracts from it. When you let go of the mediocre, you make space for brilliance to rise. Nothing is ever truly lost; what you eliminate falls back into your creative well, a resource for your future. Editing isn't a loss—it's a gain.

So how do you begin? Start by identifying the weakest parts of your work. Be honest with yourself: Which elements feel out of place? Which ideas aren't fully realized? Which parts, if removed, would make the whole stronger? Then, let them go. Trust that the space they leave behind will fill with something better.

And here's the secret: The more you practice this, the easier it becomes. Over time, you'll develop a sharper sense of what belongs and what doesn't. You'll start to see your work with greater clarity, and you'll find yourself drawn less to adding and more to refining. This isn't just a creative habit; it's a creative mindset.

Creativity isn't just about what you include—it's about what you leave out. Steve Jobs let go of complexity to create simplicity. Twyla Tharp cut away excess to reveal movement. Coco Chanel rejected the overdecorated to craft elegance. In every case, the act of subtraction wasn't an afterthought; it was the work itself.

As you refine your ability to subtract, you'll discover a new level of clarity.

Once I've stripped away the mediocre, how do I turn what remains into something achievable?

21

PRACTICE THE ART OF THE POSSIBLE

Every movie I have worked on never had enough budget or enough shooting days. It didn't matter how long the schedule was or how rich the budget. There's never enough. Even Jim Cameron, when he was making *Avatar* for $300 million, said he wished he had more money. So don't complain about what you don't have. Creativity isn't about no limits—it's about working within limits to achieve something extraordinary. The art of the possible is both practical and profound: You do what you can with what you have, and often, that's more than enough.

Constraints are inevitable. Time, budget, resources—there's always something in short supply. But limits force creatives to think more innovatively. They push you to focus on what's truly essential. Phil Hansen is a visual artist; in art school he developed an intense pointillist style. He worked with such physical severity that he developed a "career-ending" tremor because he damaged the nerves in his drawing hand. In his landmark TED Talk, *Embrace the Shake*, he explores how physical limitations led him to new artistic breakthroughs. He learned he didn't need more motor control; he needed to see what was already possible.

That's easier said than done.

It is, but practicality fuels progress. Turning ideas into action requires focusing on what's feasible. Pragmatic steps lead to real outcomes, while perfectionism and overreach can stall progress. Starting small and iterating will lead to scalable success. You don't have to wait for perfect conditions. You start where you are and build from there.

Rinde Eckert, one of the greatest living vocalists—his range is unparalleled; his collaborations range from avant-garde Kronos Quartet to jazz guitarist Bill Frisell—is also a musical savant. He can pick up any instrument, even one he's never held before, and play it almost instantly. His favorite instruments? Those that are broken, damaged. The physical imperfections allow him to create unique musical perfection. Tellingly, Rinde began his career in theater: Theater is a beautiful example of the benefits of constraints. Theater is all about limitations: You only have a couple of hours; the audience only sees the show from the fixed position of one seat; the stage has a specific size and shape; and there's not much money. Yet through these limitations, theater is infinite—it can bring you to a single room or an entire battlefield, compress or extend time, be in one location or everywhere.

How do I know what's possible for me?

Start with what you have. Take stock of your skills, time, and tools. Instead of fixating on what's missing, identify what's available. Do this simple exercise: Create a "Possibility Inventory." List everything at your disposal right now to move your project forward. You'll likely find you have more than you think.

What if my goals feel overwhelming?

Set realistic milestones. Break large goals into smaller, achievable steps. Focus on completing each one rather than worrying about the entire journey. Using project management tools can help structure tasks into manageable chunks. Your progress will compound when you tackle one step at a time.

There's always so much to do. How do I prioritize?

Learn to focus on what matters most. Ask yourself, "What is the one thing I can do now that will make the biggest impact?"

Celebrating small wins seems trivial. Does it really help?

Absolutely. Acknowledging progress, no matter how small, keeps momentum alive. Recognizing achievements fosters a sense of possibility and prevents burnout. Try this: At the end of each day, write down three things you accomplished. Reflecting on what you've made possible reinforces forward motion.

Creativity isn't about waiting for the stars to align—it's about making something happen with what you have right now. By practicing the art of the possible, you'll find that the limits you work within can lead to limitless results.

There's this project I worked on before, I put it aside. Could I be ready to pick it up again?

22

NO NOSTALGIA

Creativity moves forward. Always. The past is a tempting place, full of moments when everything seemed to click. But nostalgia is a mirage—it tricks you into chasing something that no longer exists. Herakleitos had it right: You cannot step into the same river. The river changes. And so do you.

The past feels safer. At least I know it worked.

That's the illusion. You believe you want to restore the work as it was. You're really longing for the person you were when you made it. And that person? Gone. You've grown. You see differently now, think differently, create differently. Trying to recapture an old spark will only leave you chasing shadows.

Miles Davis never looked back. Which made him great. *Kind of Blue* changed music forever, and he could have spent the rest of his life remaking it. But he didn't. Instead, he leaped into electric jazz, alienating critics, challenging audiences, and reshaping the sound of an era. "I have to change," he said. "It's like a curse." Maybe. Or maybe it's a gift—the refusal to stay still.

What if I want to revisit an old project?

Look at it. Learn from it. Let it remind you of how far you've come. But don't try to repeat it. That's how creativity dies, trapped in the cycle of recreating what once felt new.

David Bowie never let that happen. Reinvention wasn't a gimmick for him; it was survival. He didn't cling to old successes, no matter how beloved. Ziggy Stardust. The Thin White Duke. Berlin-era Bowie. Every time the world tried to define him, he slipped away, moving into the next version of himself before nostalgia could take hold. That's why his work still feels alive. It never stood still long enough to grow stale.

Who was influenced by Bowie's constant transformations? Madonna. Lady Gaga. Even Beyoncé. You one day.

Change is hard. The past is comfortable.

That's the challenge. But creativity doesn't live in comfort—it lives in the unknown. Every time you choose growth over repetition, you reaffirm your commitment to your craft and yourself.

If you need to, try this: Write a letter to your past creative self. Say thank you. Acknowledge what that self made possible. Honor who created the work, the you at that moment in time. Then let that version of yourself go.

Your job isn't to recreate. Your job is to make something only you, now, can and must make.

Miles didn't look back. Bowie didn't look back. Neither should you. Creativity thrives in the present. It's here, now, waiting.

Get your feet wet. Step into the river.

Should I always be working on something?

23

ALLOW FOR FALLOW TIME

Creativity moves in cycles—planting, growing, harvesting. But between those phases, there's another: rest. Just as fields need to lie fallow to regain their fertility, your creative mind needs periods of stillness to regenerate. The world tells you to keep producing, to fill every gap with work. Ignore that voice. Rest isn't indulgence. It's fuel.

Breakthroughs don't come from grinding—they come from stepping away. You've felt it before: the shower thought, the sudden insight on a walk. Creativity doesn't stop when you rest; it just moves underground, working in the dark like roots before the bloom.

Hayao Miyazaki understands this. Between films, he vanishes. No deadlines, no next project—just time spent walking, reading, staring at the sky. And then, when he returns, he makes something like *Spirited Away*. That's what fallow time does. It clears the clutter, making room for the extraordinary.

But what if I feel guilty stepping away?

That guilt? It's the productivity trap. A mind in constant motion can't reflect, can't stretch, can't wander into the unexpected. Doing nothing isn't nothing! It's an active process. Letting yourself binge a ridiculous TV show, read something frivolous, or waste an afternoon isn't a betrayal of your craft. It's compost. It breaks down, fertilizes the soil, makes new things possible.

Science backs this up. The "incubation effect" proves that stepping away leads to better problem-solving. It's why writers sleep on drafts, why musicians take breaks mid-session. If you're stuck, the best thing you can do is leave. The idea will follow.

So I should schedule breaks?

Yes. Build fallow time into your routine—an hour, a week, a season. Block it out like a meeting. Miyazaki doesn't stumble into rest; he makes space for it. So should you.

Won't I lose momentum?

This isn't about stopping—it's about trusting. Trust that your creativity won't vanish when you rest. Trust that your mind keeps working, even when it seems quiet. Keep a notebook nearby. The best ideas will find you when you're not looking for them.

What if I'm stuck. Does that mean I've lost my creativity?

24

THE RESET

Even the best creatives hit a wall. The work feels lifeless, the ideas aren't flowing, and every attempt to fix it makes things worse. It's frustrating, sometimes terrifying. But these moments aren't failures. They're signals. They're telling you it's time for a reset.

Creativity doesn't move in a straight line. It spirals through cycles—expansion, contraction, renewal. Reframe the way you think about "stuck." It's an invitation to evolve.

I get stuck all the time. Creative problems feel like being locked inside yourself. The reset gives you a different awareness, turns you and the problem inside out, so you can sense the world fresh with new eyes.

David Bowie mastered the art of the reset. After *Ziggy Stardust,* he could have coasted forever as a glam-rock icon. Instead, he dismantled the persona completely and dove into the raw, experimental sounds of the *Berlin Trilogy*. Critics were baffled. Some fans were disappointed. But Bowie understood that staying still was the real risk. He once said, "If you feel safe in the area you're working in, you're not working in the right area." Every reinvention pushed him into new creative territory. Each reset wasn't just survival—it was evolution.

I don't want to abandon my work. What else can I do?

You could adjust how you express yourself in another medium. Vera Wang, the daughter of Chinese immigrants, grew up in New York City.

She set her sights on being a figure skater, competing professionally through her teens, but her dreams were dashed when she and her partner didn't qualify in the Nationals. She had to reset. She took her passion for form and poise and became the senior fashion editor at *Vogue* at the age of 23. When she was 40, she started her line of bridal gowns. Her well-known work was shaped by the reset.

What's the best way to reset?

First, stop forcing it. You can't think your way out of creative stagnation—you have to *disrupt* it. Step back. Change direction. Try something completely outside your medium. If you're a writer, paint. If you're a filmmaker, play music. You don't have to be good at it. The point is to shake up your creative instincts and see what emerges.

Change your environment. Work from a park or a café instead of your usual space. Travel, even if it's just to the next town over. Rearrange your studio. Shift the conditions, and your mind will follow.

But most importantly, reconnect with *why* you create. Strip away the pressure, the expectations, the fear of failure, and get back to what drew you to this work in the first place. Write it, sing it, dance it. Let it ground you.

A reset isn't an ending; it's a beginning. A redirect. It's a chance to reframe your work, refresh your vision, remind yourself what matters. Creativity doesn't just need time and space. It needs a new way of seeing.

Redirecting feels like giving up.

25

THE REDIRECT

Sometimes the door is locked. No matter how hard you push, nothing budges. The instinct is to keep pressing forward, to force the breakthrough. But what if, instead of battering the door down, you find a side entrance? A big part of creative persistence is knowing when to pivot; in start-ups, we pivot all the time. A well-timed redirect, whether it's a small sidestep or a complete creative bank shot, can unlock new ideas and reignite your flow.

Redirecting is a strategy. It's recognizing that if the direct path isn't working, there's often a better way through. Some of the best creative breakthroughs come not from hammering away at a problem but from stepping sideways into something unexpected. When you shift your focus—even temporarily—you create space for new insights to emerge.

Sometimes you redirect yourself; sometimes redirection is thrust upon you. From the beginnings of their careers, the Wachowskis held the passion that became *The Matrix,* but the scale of *The Matrix* was so large that financiers wouldn't trust them. So the Wachowskis made *Bound* first—a low-budget film noir that transcended its genre and proved their skills. That redirect convinced the money-people and got their signature movie made.

Won't I lose momentum if I shift my focus?

Momentum doesn't always have to be in a straight line. Think of it like jazz: Sometimes, the most interesting things happen in the improvisation. Billie Eilish and her brother, Finneas, know this well. When a song isn't working, they don't force it. They play. They experiment. The song *"bad guy"* started as a detour, a playful tangent. That freedom led them somewhere new—somewhere they wouldn't have reached if they'd just kept pushing the same idea.

Redirection keeps you moving, but in a way that feels alive rather than forced. It allows you to loosen your grip just enough for something fresh to break through.

How do I make a redirect work for me?

Step into a side project, something that feels light, playful, with low stakes. Make it an experiment. Or try flipping your perspective: What would your project look like if you approached it in the opposite way? Constraints can also be surprisingly liberating—set a challenge for yourself, like creating something in one day or with a limited palette of ideas.

Collaboration is another way to redirect. Talking through your creative roadblock with someone outside your field—an artist speaking with a scientist, a filmmaker with a musician—can reveal angles you hadn't considered. When creative energy gets stuck, sometimes the best way to loosen it is to borrow energy from another discipline.

But what if even a redirect doesn't shake things loose? What if I feel like there's nothing left to give, that my well has run dry?

26

WHEN YOU RUN OUT OF IDEAS

There's a particular kind of dread that sets in when your mind feels empty. You stare at the page, the canvas, the blank screen, and... nothing. No flicker of inspiration, no sudden spark. Just silence. And with that silence comes fear.

Yes. I wonder what if I'm done? What if I'll never have another idea?

Running out of ideas isn't the end. It's part of the process. It's a sign that you've been working hard, and your creative mind needs a reset. The key isn't to panic—it's to change your approach.

Does this mean I've used up my creativity?

Creativity isn't a finite resource, and you can't "use it up." It's a skill, a muscle, and just like any muscle, it needs to be worked in different ways to stay strong.

Pixar understands this. When a story isn't working, they don't sit idly and hope something happens. They gather their Braintrust—a team of filmmakers who throw out dozens of ideas, most of which will never make it to the final cut. But that's the point. The goal isn't to get it right immediately. The goal is to generate *enough* ideas to find the one that works.

But what if everything I think of is bad?

Linus Pauling, a two-time Nobel laureate, said it well: "The best way to have a good idea is to have a lot of ideas." Even the bad ones. Creativity thrives on volume. The more ideas you generate, the better your chances of finding something great.

When the well feels dry, start by brainstorming without judgment. Set a timer for ten minutes and write down every idea that comes to mind—no matter how ridiculous. Bad ideas, silly ideas, impossible ideas. Sometimes the best ideas come from the weirdest places.

What else can help?

Shift your perspective. Ask yourself: How would a child solve this? Or ask: What would this idea look like if it were completely reversed? Shake up your usual thinking patterns. If you're stuck in words, try sketching. If you're stuck visually, try describing your idea out loud. The simple act of switching mediums can unlock something new.

Collaboration can also break the deadlock. Talk to a friend or a trusted peer. Bounce ideas around with no pressure to get it right. The missing piece of your puzzle might be something they say in passing.

And if nothing works?

Step away. Play. Doodle, build with LEGO, do a mindless task. Playfulness unlocks parts of your brain that structured thinking can't reach. Try asking ridiculous "What if?" questions: What if this had to work underwater? What if it had to fit inside a shoebox? Playfulness removes the pressure of making something "good" and replaces it with curiosity.

Once you've generated ideas, don't expect instant clarity. Let the ideas sit. Come back later, highlight a few that intrigue you, and explore from there.

Running out of ideas isn't failure—it's an invitation. It's a signal to stretch your creative process in a new direction. The spark will return. It always does.

But what if the block isn't just about ideas? What if it feels deeper—something fundamental, something that won't shake loose no matter what I try?

27

THE CURE FOR CREATIVE BLOCKS

Creative blocks feel solid, like walls towering in front of you. Look closer: They are shadows. They only seem immovable when you stand still. The longer you wait for inspiration to strike, the bigger they grow. The cure? It's deceptively simple: Stop waiting, lower your expectations, and do *something*. Action, no matter how small, is the antidote to inertia.

I feel stuck, like nothing I do will be good enough.

That's perfectionism talking. And perfectionism is the best friend of creative blocks—it feeds them, keeps them comfortable. The belief that every word, every brushstroke, every idea must be brilliant before it even exists is what freezes you in place.

Just keep going, keep going, write what Anne Lamott calls the "shitty first draft." (Have you read *Bird by Bird*?) In that mess you're making, if you persist, will be something worthwhile.

When Maya Angelou hit a creative block, she would sit on a hotel bed and play solitaire. Until her creative mind reawakened. "Sometimes after that," she said, "I've got two pages worth looking at, sometimes I've got 20." She kept the door open. And eventually, through that persistence, something real and powerful emerged. Because she refused to stop moving, the block didn't win.

But what if I don't even know where to start?

Start by lowering the bar. Write one sentence instead of an entire chapter. Sketch for two minutes instead of an hour. Hum a random melody with no plan. The goal isn't to make something great—it's to get unstuck.

Sarah Elgart, a gifted dancer and choreographer, sees creativity as a discipline. She doesn't stand still waiting for inspiration to strike—she starts moving. A warm-up stretch, a simple step sequence, anything to engage the body. It's the motion that creates momentum. One step leads to another, and before she knows it, she's dancing.

That's how all creativity works. You don't wait to feel inspired to act. You act first, and the inspiration follows.

But what if I try, and everything still feels wrong?

Then make it wrong on purpose. Set a timer for fifteen minutes and create the worst version of your idea. Write the messiest paragraph, draw the most ridiculous sketch, play the most chaotic music. When the pressure of being "good" disappears, so does the block. You're free to play, and playfulness is what leads to breakthroughs.

As Michelle Ashford, a screenwriter I have had the honor to work with, once told me, "When you're in trouble writing, write your way out of it."

What if I'm stuck in one medium?

Switch. Write in a notebook instead of typing. Use a crayon instead of a pen. Change your tools, your setting, your method. Shake up your routine so your brain has to engage in a new way.

Creative blocks only hold power if you stand still. The second you take action—any action—the block starts to dissolve. Progress beats perfection every time. Start small, stay playful, and trust that creativity will meet you on the other side.

And once you're unstuck, the next challenge isn't about generating ideas—it's about knowing which ones are worth pursuing.

How can I decide if a project will be worth my time?

28

SHOULD YOU START A NEW PROJECT?

Passion and curiosity are your fuel. Passion keeps you going when things get tough, and curiosity keeps the work from becoming stale. The best projects have both—they light a fire inside you *and* make you want to explore. If an idea excites you and makes you ask "What happens if I follow this?," that's a good sign.

But passion alone isn't enough, is it?

Passion isn't enough. Practicality matters, too. A great idea still needs an audience. It needs timing. It needs a reason to exist beyond your enthusiasm. Before I commit to producing a film, I run through an internal checklist. First, do I like the people I'll be working with? Filmmaking is collaborative—if the team isn't right, the project won't work. Second, do I believe in the story? If I don't feel it in my gut, I won't bring my best to it. Third, can I make a difference? If my involvement won't improve the project, there's no point in me being there. And finally, will an audience connect with it? Movies are meant to be seen. If I don't believe the story will resonate, I walk away.

Those are my filters. Yours may be different, but the principle remains: Your time and energy are valuable. Choose wisely.

What if I'm unsure?

Reese Witherspoon had a clear filter when she started her production company, Hello Sunshine. She saw a gap—Hollywood wasn't making enough stories about women, by women, for women. She didn't just want to produce films; she wanted to reshape the landscape. *Big Little Lies* and *The Morning Show* weren't just passion projects; they filled a need in the marketplace. She combined her creative instincts with smart strategy.

That's what you want to do. A project should excite you *and* make sense. It should feel like something only you can do, but also something people *want* you to do.

So how do I decide if a project is worth starting?

Start by checking in with yourself. Does this idea energize you? Do you have the time, focus, and resources to commit to it? Is there an audience for it? Does it align with where you want to go creatively? If you're choosing between multiple ideas, write down your thoughts. Seeing them in front of you can bring clarity.

What if I love the idea but don't know if it's viable?

Test it. Start small. Give yourself thirty days to play with the idea—sketch it out, write a rough draft, make a prototype. Exploration without full commitment lets you gather evidence. Sometimes an idea sounds exciting in theory but loses its spark when you sit down to work on it. Other times, an idea that seemed small at first keeps pulling you in. That's how you know it has legs.

If you're deciding between projects, think about balance. Are you refining something you already know how to do, or pushing into new territory? Both have value, but they require different levels of risk. The best projects stretch you just enough to grow—without overwhelming you.

Starting a project is like planting a seed. It needs the right conditions to take root. Passion, curiosity, and practicality must align. When they do, that's your signal to begin.

But not every journey lasts forever. Sometimes you need to walk away.

It feels wrong to leave something unfinished.

29

WHEN TO PUT A PROJECT ASIDE

Sometimes, the best way to move forward is to step back, pause, and let a project rest. This isn't failure; it's wisdom. Creative work isn't a straight road—it's a shifting landscape. Projects evolve, energy wanes, and priorities shift. Knowing when to put something aside frees you to focus on what truly matters.

Not all projects are meant to reach completion. Some exist to teach you something. Some are stepping stones to better ideas. Some are just experiments, exercises in stretching your creative muscles. The real mistake isn't stopping—it's forcing something that no longer serves you.

But how do I know if I should keep going?

Energy and passion are your best indicators. If a project still excites you, if there are moments when you lose yourself in the work, that's a sign to keep pushing. This is *flow*—that state where creativity feels effortless, where time disappears. But if it feels like you're dragging it forward, if every step feels heavier than the last, it may be time to reassess. If you've lost the flow completely, if you can't remember the last time the work felt alive, that's your signal.

Sometimes, the reason to pause is practical. Deadlines shift. Market conditions change. Resources dry up. There's no shame in pressing pause when external realities demand it. Creativity thrives when you focus on the right things. Not everything.

Letting go still feels like failure.

It isn't. Lin-Manuel Miranda wrote *Bring It On: The Musical* before *Hamilton*. It was a fun, moderately successful project, but it wasn't the work that defined him. He could have kept trying to make it bigger, but instead, he let it go and focused on *Hamilton*—a project that would transform his career. *Bring It On* wasn't a mistake. It was a stepping-stone. And sometimes, that's exactly what a project is meant to be.

So, how do I know when to step away?

Ask yourself: Does this project still excite me, or is it draining me? Think about the last time you felt fully engaged with the work. What made it exciting? If that spark is completely gone, it might be time to step back.

What if I feel guilty about stopping?

Reframe the project's purpose. Maybe it wasn't meant to be finished, but it still served you. Write down what you've learned from it—skills, insights, ideas that might fuel your next project. Recognizing its value, even unfinished, makes it easier to let go.

And remember, setting something aside isn't the same as discarding it. Keep a "paused projects" list. Set a reminder to revisit them in a few months. Some projects come back to life when you least expect it, with new energy and new perspective.

Pausing a project isn't giving up—it's making space. Space for work that excites you. Space for what matters most. Every project, finished or not, adds to your creative journey.

I don't know when something is finished. I always feel like my work could be better.

30

IS IT FINISHED (ENOUGH)?

There's a truism in the movie business: Movies aren't finished, they're taken away. I still think about a scene in *March of the Penguins* that I wish I could change. (It's when the baby chick dies—I wish we had written a line for Morgan Freeman to help us through.) But at some point, every creative project must be released—because it's finished enough.

The feeling that a piece of work could be better never really goes away. Creative work rarely matches the perfect version you imagined. It's a little rough, a little raw, almost there but not quite. And yet, there comes a moment when you have to let it go.

Perfection is the great trap. It whispers that one more tweak, one more pass, one more revision will finally make it flawless. But perfection is an illusion. Paul Valéry said that a creative work is never finished, "it is only abandoned." There's always more you could do, but at some point, more isn't better—it's just different.

But what if I regret releasing something before it's ready?

Most creatives feel this at some point. But external forces often dictate when a piece is done—deadlines, budgets, or sheer necessity. That's okay. Deadlines, whether set by someone else or by you, force you to finish. When I work on a movie, it is constantly evolving; we are fixing sound, adjusting music, making sure the titles are right, up until the last possible moment. At some point, though, the film has to be locked, set, and sent to theaters. The work must leave the creator's hands.

Ridley Scott's *Blade Runner* is the perfect example. The film has had multiple versions—Director's Cuts, Final Cuts, re-releases with alternate endings. But the original 1982 theatrical version, despite Scott's frustrations, became a beloved classic. The fact that he later revised it doesn't mean the first version wasn't worth releasing—it means creative work lives in an ongoing dialogue between artist and audience.

How do I know if my work is ready to share?

It will never be perfect, but it can be ready. Over time, you develop an instinct for when something is as good as it can be under the circumstances. That's the moment to release it. If you're unsure, seek input from trusted collaborators—people who can see the work clearly when your own judgment starts to blur. Sharing your work, even when it feels unfinished, creates connection and opens the door for growth.

So how do you decide if it's finished enough? Start by defining what "finished" means for this project. Is it meeting its core purpose? Does it feel complete within its own structure? Set a checklist of what *done* looks like, and when those criteria are met, trust that it's time to move forward.

Deadlines make me nervous.

That's because they force a choice. But deadlines are your ally. If you don't have one, make one. Commit to a date when you'll share the work, at whatever point it is. Deadlines push you from endless refinement into action. And when in doubt, show it before you feel ready. Sharing an unfinished piece with a trusted peer or a small audience can help you see it more clearly.

Above all, learn to let go. Tell yourself, "This is the best I can do right now," and release it. Accept that imperfection is part of the process. The world doesn't need perfect work—it needs honest work, work that reflects the moment it was created in.

The act of releasing your work isn't just about sharing. It frees you for what comes next.

What comes next?

31

LOVE WHAT YOU DO

Creativity demands your heart. If you don't love what you do—truly love it—it will show. This lack of love will seep into your work, dull your energy, and linger in your life as frustration or regret. But when you create with love, that love becomes part of the work itself. It shines through, connects with others, and sustains you, even when the road gets tough.

But love alone doesn't guarantee success.

No, but it's what keeps you going. The creative journey is filled with rejection, self-doubt, and long, uncertain stretches where nothing seems to be working. If you don't love what you're doing, it's hard to keep showing up. Love gives you the resilience to push through challenges, to keep creating when no one's watching, when the response isn't what you hoped for, when the finish line feels far away.

When I create something, how do I know if love is coming through?

You feel it. And so does everyone else. Maya Angelou said, "People will forget what you said, people will forget what you did, but they will never forget how you made them feel." That's what love does—it transmits. It turns technical skill into art. It's what makes a piece of music linger in someone's heart, what makes a film stay with them long after the credits roll. When love is in the work, you can feel it.

Hayao Miyazaki embodies this. His films—*My Neighbor Totoro, Spirited Away, Princess Mononoke*—carry an unmistakable warmth, a deep reverence for storytelling. He refuses to cut corners. When faster, cheaper animation techniques became available, he stuck with painstaking hand-drawn animation. That's his jam. He loves the craft. That's why his films endure. That's why people return to them, generation after generation.

What if I'm feeling disconnected from my creative passion?

Start by remembering why you chose this in the first place. What first drew you to your craft? When was the last time you felt completely alive in the act of creating? Write it down. Sometimes, just reflecting on that initial spark can reignite it.

Protect the joy in your work. It's easy to get caught up in deadlines, expectations, financial pressures. But those things aren't *the work*. Dedicate time to projects that exist purely for you—no audience, no market, just curiosity. These passion projects often become the most meaningful, for you and for the people who experience them.

Align your work with what you care about. When new opportunities come up, ask: Does this reflect my values? Does it excite me? If your answer is no, think twice. Saying "no" to the wrong projects is just as important as saying "yes" to the right ones.

You won't love every moment. No creator does. But if you love the work itself—the deep, essential process of creating—then that love will carry you through. It will give your work vitality. And in turn, it will connect you to the people who need to experience it.

Because ultimately, loving what you do isn't just about you. It's about the people you serve, the audience that finds meaning in your work.

But isn't creativity about self-expression first?

32

LOVE WHO YOU DO IT FOR

Creativity is an act of connection. Just as a marriage is meaningless without a partner, your creative enterprise is meaningless without its recipients. Your audience, your collaborators, your clients—they complete the circle. When you create with love for the people who will experience your work, something shifts. The work gains purpose, resonance, and the potential to leave a lasting impact.

Connection makes your work stronger. Creativity isn't a one-way street; it's an exchange. You create, your audience responds, and that response fuels your next creation. When you truly see and value your audience, your work deepens. It's about respect. Great work meets people where they are, not where you wish they were.

I get that, but how do I feel that connection?

I feel it every time I teach my MBA students at UC Berkeley. They walk into my class with sharp intellects, giant ambitions, and also deep vulnerability. Many of them fear they can't connect, that their voices won't land, that their ideas won't translate into leadership. I love teaching them because I love what they represent: the next generation of decision-makers who will shape industries, economies, and lives.

When I'm in the room with them, my focus shifts entirely to their needs: What will help them grow? What will unlock their confidence? I see them wrestle with new skills, push past their fears, and, by the end, walk out with a firmer sense of their own voice. That's what makes my work meaningful. It's a relationship. The more I invest in them, the more their engagement inspires me in return.

How do I cultivate that kind of connection with my audience?

Start by getting to know them. Who are they? What do they hope to feel or experience from your work? Imagine you are creating for a specific person; see their face as you make your work. Sometimes I actually tape a photo of someone in front of my laptop, so I can look into their eyes while I'm writing. So they are not an abstract demographic. So I can ask: What does this person struggle with? What excites them? What do they *need* right now?

Shift your mindset from self-expression to service. Yes, your creativity is personal. But it's also an act of generosity. Ask yourself: How does my work help? What does it offer? Write down three ways your next project might impact someone. That simple shift in focus can transform how you approach your work.

Engage with your audience. Even though it can be scary. Listen to their feedback, their interpretations, their stories. I am not suggesting you chase their approval, but it is important for you to understand the *relationship* between your work and the people who experience it. Whether through conversations, comments, or quiet observation, let that connection guide you.

Loving your audience doesn't mean giving them exactly what they want. It means giving them your best. It means creating with care, thoughtfulness, and respect for their intelligence and humanity. When you love who you do it for, your work carries more weight. It lingers. It matters.

But creativity is rarely a solo endeavor. Who you work with—your collaborators, partners, and teams—can elevate or derail your projects.

Right. But. How can I discern who to collaborate with? So they share my vision, my values, even some of my love?

33

MARRY WISELY (CHOOSING YOUR COLLABORATORS)

The right collaborator can take your work to new heights. The wrong one can sink the entire ship. Creativity thrives on partnership, but collaboration isn't just about talent—it's about trust, respect, and shared vision. And just like marriage, it's wise to date before you say "I do."

Collaboration is foundational to great work. The most enduring creative achievements—films, albums, businesses—are the result of strong partnerships. The Wright brothers didn't just share DNA; they shared a relentless problem-solving mindset that led to human flight. At Pixar, storytelling, animation, and sound design come together in a seamless blend, proving that the right mix of perspectives creates something far greater than what one person could achieve alone.

So, it's always better to collaborate than to work alone?

Not necessarily. A bad partnership will drain your energy, muddle your vision, and slow progress to a crawl. No collaborator is better than the wrong collaborator.

Compatibility matters more than raw talent. Shared values, work ethic, and communication styles will carry a collaboration through inevitable rough patches. Aligned values foster trust, which is the foundation of any long-term partnership. The best collaborators aren't always the most skilled—they're the ones who push you, challenge you, and support you when the work gets hard.

When do you know someone isn't the right fit?

You know early. As my business mentor said, "Hire slow, fire fast." I once worked with a writer whose talent was undeniable. The project was solid, the potential was huge. But when tough conversations arose—about deadlines, rewrites, and creative direction—they disappeared. I trusted my instincts and walked away. Later, I saw the same patterns repeat in their other collaborations. That experience reinforced a key truth: Talent is just one part of the equation. Compatibility—how someone works under pressure, how they communicate, how they handle feedback—is what makes or breaks a collaboration.

Beyoncé and Jay-Z, collaborators in life and work, understand this. Their creative and business collaborations serve them because they respect each other's strengths and share a clear vision. But even they don't commit blindly. They experiment, test ideas, recalibrate.

Okay, so how do I find the right collaborator?

Start with a test run. Work on something small together before committing to a big project. It doesn't have to be high stakes—just enough to see how you both handle feedback, pressure, and problem-solving. If you find yourself constantly having to accommodate someone else's disorganization, poor communication, or lack of follow-through, that's a sign to walk away.

Setting expectations feels uncomfortable.

It's far more uncomfortable when things go wrong. Be explicit about roles, responsibilities, and deadlines from the beginning. Assumptions lead to resentment. Write down what success looks like for both of you. If you're working on a long-term project, consider a simple collaboration agreement. Clarity at the start prevents major headaches later.

Don't let talent blind you to red flags. A brilliant partner who lacks respect, reliability, or resilience will do more harm than good. How someone responds to feedback is one of the best predictors of long-term compatibility. If they shut down, get defensive, or resist compromise, that could be your early warning sign.

What if I ignore my gut and move forward anyway?

You'll regret it. If something feels off, listen to it. The longer you stay in a bad collaboration, the harder it is to leave. Write down your nonnegotiables—respect, accountability, creative alignment, whatever they are—and use that list as your guide.

The best collaborators are like the best spouses: They challenge you, support you, and make you better. Choose wisely, date before you commit, and trust that the right partnership will elevate your entire creative life.

Sounds like I'll have to talk a lot about my creative work. I don't want to have to explain myself.

34

HOW TO TALK ABOUT YOUR LIFE AND WORK

Being a creative isn't just about making things. It's about navigating conversations with people who may not understand, appreciate, or share your path. How you talk about your creative life shapes how others see you and how you see yourself. Each conversation is an opportunity to reinforce your purpose, build understanding, and strengthen connections.

The language you use matters. When you speak confidently about your creative life, you're explaining what you do and affirming it for yourself. Downplaying your work or speaking defensively diminishes its perceived value, both to others and within your own mind. If you don't take yourself seriously, why should anyone else?

I hate explaining what I do. People either don't get it or think it's not a "real" job.

Confidence is key. If you frame your work as uncertain or unimportant, people will reflect that uncertainty back at you. The way you present your creative life sets the tone for how others respond.

Navigating conversations with other creatives brings its own set of challenges. The world loves rankings—awards, followers, financial success—but creativity isn't a competition. The most meaningful creative conversations happen when you stay grounded in your own journey instead of measuring yourself against someone else's. It's easy to compare, but comparison rarely fuels good work. The more secure you are in what you do, the easier it is to celebrate others without questioning yourself.

Talking about my work with family is even harder. They just don't get it.

Many creatives face this. Parents, relatives, or friends with more traditional careers may struggle to see the value of creative work. Instead of trying to justify yourself, reframe your work in ways they understand—commitment, discipline, problem-solving. You don't need their approval, but bridging the gap can make conversations easier.

I first met Taika Waititi early in his career, when we selected him to join the All Roads project at National Geographic, an initiative that brought together filmmakers from different cultures from around the world. Taika faced skepticism about his filmmaking style because he blended darkness with humor. But that was his genius. He leaned into humor and storytelling, reframing his work as a way to preserve culture and identity. He didn't need everyone to understand—he just needed enough people to believe in his vision. That belief carried him from indie films to Marvel blockbusters.

How do I explain my work to different people without sounding like I'm bragging—or apologizing?

Start by being clear, not tentative, not defensive. Speak about your work with the same ease you'd describe any other profession. "I'm working on a new script about..." is far stronger than, "Oh, it's just this little thing I'm trying..." Prepare a short, confident way to describe what you do, and practice saying it until it feels natural.

Tailor your language to your audience. Noncreatives don't need technical details—they want to understand why your work matters. When talking with peers, lean into shared experiences. With anyone, focus on your passion, your process, and your curiosity. People connect with purpose more than with specifics.

And when those conversations happen with other creatives, take the opportunity to build bridges. It's tempting to compare careers, but every creative journey unfolds differently. If someone else is succeeding, let it inspire you instead of making you feel small. "It's exciting to see where your work is going" fosters connection in a way that comparison never will.

Should I be honest about my struggles, or will that make me seem unprofessional?

Honesty builds trust—when framed as part of growth. Creative struggles are inevitable, but how you talk about them matters. Saying, "I'm figuring out my next steps right now," keeps the conversation open-ended. Own both the highs and the lows. The more you normalize the realities of creative life, the easier it is to stay grounded in your own journey.

Talking about your work is part of the work itself. Speak with clarity, confidence, and curiosity. The more you own your story, the easier it becomes to share, no matter who's listening.

But sometimes, the people listening won't cheer for you. Envy—whether subtle or overt—can complicate creative relationships.

That's for sure. I had one piece that worked, a minor success, and now some of my friends won't talk to me!

35

JEALOUSY FROM PEERS AND FRIENDS

Success is a gift, but it comes with challenges—and one of the hardest is navigating the jealousy it can evoke in those closest to you. Friends who once cheered for you might grow quieter. Peers who once supported you might become distant or critical. Jealousy isn't always loud. Sometimes, it's a subtle undercurrent that shifts the dynamic of a relationship. How you handle it can shape those relationships and also your peace of mind.

I didn't expect friends to act differently just because things are going well for me.

Jealousy can be surprising. You expect success to bring celebration. But jealousy is rarely about you—it's about the person feeling it. Insecurity, self-doubt, and comparison have a way of creeping in, making your achievements feel like reminders of their struggles. That's why jealousy often shows up in backhanded compliments, passive-aggressive remarks, or a noticeable silence when you share good news. "You're so lucky," they might say. Or "Must be nice to have everything handed to you." Or maybe they just stop responding. Recognizing these signals early helps you respond thoughtfully instead of reacting emotionally.

So what do I do? Ignore it? Call it out?

How you respond matters. The best approach is a mix of empathy and confidence. Getting defensive or shrinking yourself won't help, but neither will pretending it isn't happening. Acknowledge the emotions at play, but don't apologize for your success.

Mindy Kaling's rise in the comedy world came with its share of jealousy. Early in her career, as she moved from writer to performer to showrunner, some peers didn't take her seriously. There were subtle jabs, cold shoulders, and dismissive comments. But instead of letting it shake her, she stayed focused on her work. She didn't downplay her success, but she also didn't let it define her relationships. Over time, her consistency and humility turned skeptics into supporters. That's the key: Keep doing the work, and let time do the rest.

But I don't want to feel guilty for doing well.

You shouldn't feel guilty. When someone you care about struggles with jealousy, you can acknowledge their feelings without diminishing your own success. A simple statement like, "I know things might feel tough for you right now, but I really admire the work you're doing," validates them without making you smaller.

If jealousy becomes toxic, boundaries are essential. Some people process their emotions and move forward. Others hold on to resentment, letting it turn into bitterness. If a friend repeatedly undermines you or makes you feel like you have to hide your achievements, it may be time for some distance. A direct but kind approach—"I value our friendship, but I'd love for us to support each other without comparison"—can help reset the relationship.

Maybe I should just stop talking about my work.

Muting yourself to protect someone else's feelings won't serve either of you. Instead, focus on gratitude. When sharing successes, acknowledge the people who have helped you along the way. A statement like, "I've had amazing opportunities, and I'm grateful for the people who've supported me," reminds others that success is rarely a solo effort.

You can also redirect the conversation. Ask about their work, their passions, their goals. "I know you've been working on something exciting, too—tell me about it." Jealousy thrives on isolation. When you turn a moment of comparison into a moment of connection, it often shifts the energy.

Ultimately, jealousy from peers and friends is more about their internal struggles than about your success. You can't control their feelings, but you can control how you respond. Lead with kindness. Set boundaries when needed. Stay focused on your work. The ones who are meant to be in your life will come around.

And yet, dealing with jealousy from peers is only part of the challenge. Talking about your creative work with life partners and family members requires a different kind of care and clarity.

My partner and my family should just understand, right?

36

COMMUNICATING WITH PARTNERS AND FAMILY

No creative journey happens in isolation. If you share your life with a partner or family, they're part of your world, too, whether they understand your creative process or not. Communicating your needs isn't just about protecting your work. It's about building a shared life that honors everyone's contributions, including your own.

Supportive partners and family want to help, but they usually need some coaching. To them, the rhythms and demands of a creative life can feel confusing. "Why do you say, 'I'm still working on the project,' even while we're eating dinner?" they wonder. "Why can't you just work at home, why do you need to go to your special place?" they ask. If you don't explain your process, they may misinterpret it as selfishness or disinterest, even when that's far from the truth.

It still feels like I'm asking for too much.

If you need dedicated time to work, that doesn't mean you love your family any less. We need focused, uninterrupted time for meaningful creative output. The more your loved ones understand that your creative work isn't a hobby but is a serious commitment, the more likely they are to respect and support it.

How do I even start that conversation?

Start by explaining your creative process. Share why you need time, space, or quiet. Be specific, and use language that helps them understand the stakes. "When I'm in the middle of writing, even a quick interruption can pull me out of my train of thought," you might say. "Having a set time to work without distractions really helps me do my best work."

Be clear about your needs. If you need three hours on Saturday mornings to focus, say so. Balance that with a commitment to spend time together afterward. This reinforces that your work matters, but so do they.

What if they feel like I'm choosing my work over them?

Appreciation goes a long way. Recognize their support while making your requests. "I'm so grateful for how you encourage me," you might say. "It would mean a lot if you could help me carve out time for my work by handling dinner tonight." Framing your needs with gratitude helps them feel part of your creative journey rather than sidelined by it.

For partners and family members who want to support you, offer guidance. Encourage curiosity about your process, but discourage critiques disguised as questions. "Why are you doing it that way?" can be rephrased as, "Tell me more about your process." Likewise, expressions of encouragement like "I'm proud of you for working so hard" feel far more supportive than "I can't wait to see what you make!" which can unintentionally add pressure.

A shared calendar can also help. If your creative time is visibly scheduled—just like a work meeting or a doctor's appointment—your family is more likely to respect it.

Supportive relationships thrive on clear communication. By helping your loved ones understand your creative world—and by valuing their efforts to support you—you build a bridge of mutual respect. This foundation enriches both your work and your life together.

Okay. But I have a full-time day job. I do my creative work after that. How can I balance my relationships, my day job, and my creative work?

37

FEEDING CREATIVE LIFE EVEN WHEN IT IS NOT YOUR PRIMARY LIFE

Not everyone has the luxury of making creativity the center of their world. Maybe you have a demanding job, a family to care for, responsibilities that claim your best hours. Does that mean your creative life has to shrink, subside, shrivel, waiting for some future day when the conditions are perfect?

It does not. Creativity doesn't need to dominate your schedule to thrive—it just needs to be fed. Even in small doses, even in stolen moments. Before Toni Morrison became the literary giant we revere today, she worked full time as an editor and raised her children alone. Her writing time? The early morning hours before her household woke up. In those minutes, she wrote *The Bluest Eye*. She didn't wait for more time. She worked with what she had.

That sounds impossible. I barely have time as it is.

Creativity survives on consistency. You don't need three uninterrupted hours—you need twenty minutes. James Clear's *Atomic Habits* proves that small, deliberate actions compound over time. Write one paragraph. Sketch one rough idea. Hum out a melody on your commute. The goal isn't to finish something—it's to keep the wheels turning.

But my day job drains me.

It might, but it can also feed you. Creative sparks come from unexpected places. A frustrating meeting. A conversation overheard in line at the grocery store. The patterns on a rain-soaked window. Keep a small notebook or a notes app to catch these moments. Your creative self is always collecting, even when you're not actively working.

Still, how do I make time when everything else is a priority?

If you never give creativity a seat at the table, it will always be fighting for scraps. The trick isn't finding time; it's making time. Block out short, focused sessions, even just twenty-five minutes. Set a timer. Treat it like an appointment that can't be canceled. The key is to show up regularly, even in small ways.

That means saying "no" to other things.

You can't say "yes" to everything and expect your creative life to survive. If your evenings are sacred for writing, don't give them away to mindless scrolling or obligations you don't truly want. Saying "no" to something unimportant is saying "yes" to your creative self.

Even between projects, you can keep your creative mind active. Watch a film that wakes up your senses. Read a book that challenges you. Walk through a museum with no agenda. These "creative snacks" keep your fire burning even when you're not producing.

So I don't have to wait for the perfect time?

The perfect time doesn't exist. The myth of perfect conditions is a trap that keeps people from ever starting. Your creative life can exist in the margins—early mornings, late nights, lunch breaks, even the seconds between tasks. Morrison's mornings were imperfect, yet they created a masterpiece. Your moments, however brief, can do the same.

I don't want brief. I am ambitious—not for myself, really. For everyone, for the people I can share with, for what my work can bring to the world. I want to make the narratives you talk about, narratives that forge a path forward.

38

FOOD FOR YOUR CREATIVE TABLE

Creativity isn't a faucet you can turn on whenever you need it. It's a living force—one that requires care, attention, and constant nourishment. Ignore it for too long, and it dims. Feed it well, and it grows brighter, stronger, more surprising.

Think of your creativity as a table you're always setting. What's on it today? Is it rich with inspiration, rest, and new experiences? Or is it bare, waiting for you to remember it exists? Julia Cameron, in *The Artist's Way*, calls this practice "artist dates"—intentional moments where you step away from your work to refill your creative cup. They don't have to be elaborate. A slow walk through a park, browsing a used bookstore, watching an old film you've never seen—these aren't indulgences. They're fuel.

But what if I don't have time?

You don't need time. You need input. Creativity feeds on novelty—new experiences, fresh ideas, unexpected connections. Exposing yourself to different perspectives keeps your brain sharp. The good news? Novelty isn't about expensive trips or dramatic changes. It's in the small things: taking a different route home, trying a dish you've never eaten, listening to new music. These micro-adjustments wake up your brain, keeping it primed for discovery.

Okay, but new experiences take effort. What about everyday fuel?

Energy and focus are the foundation of creative work. You know David Lynch, right? You should. The quintessential American surrealist. The filmmaker who created *Twin Peaks* and *Blue Velvet*. Weird as those movies are, he built his entire career on a foundation of balance. He meditated daily, wrote in journals, drew sketches, and made space for his mind to wander. In *Catching the Big Fish*, he described how ideas surface when the mind is clear—when there's room for them to emerge. Without that space, even the most vibrant imagination can become cluttered.

So what does that mean for me?

Start with daily rituals. Small cues that signal to your brain it's time to create. Lighting a candle before you write. Listening to the same song before sketching. Five minutes of free writing before a work session. These rituals are rhythm, a way of stepping into your creative space with intention.

Seek out new experiences, even in small ways. Visit an art exhibit, take a different walk, watch a film in a language you don't speak. Novelty keeps your creative well from running dry. Make a habit of experiencing something new at least once a month—you'll be surprised at how it sparks your work.

And don't underestimate rest. Sleep, physical relaxation, and mental downtime are essential. A well-rested mind is a fertile mind.

Does community matter, too?

Absolutely. Surround yourself with people who challenge and inspire you. Share your work, exchange ideas, learn from others. A strong creative community can expand your perspective and reignite your passion.

Creativity doesn't thrive on sheer willpower. It thrives when you feed it. New ideas. Quiet moments. Deep rest. A community that lifts you up. A creative life, well-tended, will always have something to offer.

But even with all this nourishment, the creative path is rarely a straight line. It winds, doubles back, and surprises you in ways that are both frustrating and beautiful.

Nonlinear? I'm not that good with nonlinear.

39

IT IS A SPIRAL

The creative life isn't a straight road. It isn't even a circle, looping you back to the same starting point. It's a spiral—widening as you move, taking you deeper into your work and your understanding of it. You'll return to familiar ideas, themes, and challenges, but each time, you'll carry more with you. More experience. More perspective. More truth.

But doesn't that feel frustrating? Like I'm just reworking the same things?

It can. It can feel like you're stuck, like you're covering the same ground over and over. But repetition is evolution. Your rituals, like morning writing or afternoons at the gym, might seem repetitive at first. But over time, they open new layers of thought, revealing insights that weren't visible before. What once felt simple becomes profound through experience. The spiral refines you.

But shouldn't I always be moving forward?

You are. Just not in the way you expect. Creativity doesn't progress in a straight line. Progress builds on itself, sometimes in ways we can't see. A single project might feel isolated, but it adds to the foundation beneath you. The skills, instincts, and knowledge you gain carry into the next thing, and the next, and the next. The spiral expands as you do.

So revisiting ideas isn't a step backward?

Not at all. Look at Frida Kahlo. She painted herself over and over, exploring pain, resilience, and identity. The same face, the same themes, but each painting contained something new. More depth. More truth. She wasn't repeating herself—she was refining. Every pass brought her closer to what she was trying to say.

We often say that artists make one art, over and over again. Filmmakers make the same film. Architects design the same building. Entrepreneurs repeatedly start companies to solve the same problem. This isn't a deficit. It's how we come to know a person's signature style; that style becomes a brand; that brand builds value.

How do I embrace this in my own work?

Reframe repetition as discovery. Returning to ideas, themes, or even unfinished projects isn't a failure—it's a chance to go deeper. Pull out an old piece of work and ask yourself: What would I do differently now? What can I bring to it that I couldn't before?

Track your journey. A journal, a portfolio, even a simple folder of past projects—these let you see the shape of your creative spiral. What once felt like detours might reveal themselves as essential steps. That idea you abandoned two years ago? You might finally have what you need to finish it.

Use each return to push outward. When you find yourself circling back to a challenge or a theme, don't resist it—lean in. Ask: What can I explore here that I wasn't ready for before? The past isn't a constraint. It's a foundation.

The creative life has no final destination—only the next curve, the next layer, the next discovery. And that's the beauty of it. Write a letter to your younger creative self, reflecting on how far you've traveled outward. Recognize how each twist and turn has shaped you into the creator you are now.

Does the spiral ever end?

PART TWO

CREATIVE LIFE PRACTICUM

40

SCALING

Your life, devoted to your creative work, is an enterprise, whether you admit it or not. And every enterprise worth its sweat must grow.

Scaling is the unromantic word for a deeply romantic idea: Your work should find its people; and more people tomorrow than yesterday. The truth is, creative people often crave scale more than they admit. We want our paintings to hang in more rooms, our films to play to more audiences, our words to be quoted by more readers. Because the work was made to be experienced.

Yet many creatives stop short of the one truth that businesses know by instinct: Reach does not multiply itself. Scale must be built in, poured into the foundation of how you work and how you live. Otherwise, your reach remains accidental, depending on luck, gatekeepers, momentary trends.

If you wish to live by your work, you must treat your creative life as a living business. A business shapes its offer to the market it serves. It designs its operations to reach new audiences while caring for its old ones. It sets up protections so its value is preserved, and structures so that the creator's energy feeds the work instead of being drained by chaos.

Scaling is an act of devotion to your own purpose. Scaling says: This thing I made is worth sharing widely. It says: I trust my work can travel farther than I can walk it myself.

I do trust my work. I don't know how it can travel far.

Let's do this together. In this Practicum, we'll step fully into this mindset. You'll learn how to craft your creative practice as a resilient enterprise, capable of expanding into more markets, building more relationships, and growing income to match the value you provide.

You will see how the habits of founders, producers, lawyers, and marketers apply to the brush, the pen, the lens. Because scaling is about stepping up to meet the size of your own vision.

It's how creative life endures. And you are ready for it.

Yes. Tell me more about scaling up.

41

START-UP MINDSET

Much of what I have learned about creativity has come from my business experience. Much of my business understanding comes from my movie experience. Because every movie is a start-up.

When you make a film, you develop the idea, build the team, raise the capital, test the product, make the product, market it, distribute it, and pivot many times along the way. Perhaps my most important background in coaching start-up entrepreneurs is that I have made forty movies. Which is to say, I have a lot of pattern recognition because I have done forty start-ups.

Creativity is building something from nothing. Every project you start is an enterprise built around an idea. Whether you realize it or not, your creative life is a start-up. The most successful creatives don't just create—they test, refine, adapt, and grow.

I love making things, but business thinking feels like a different world.

It's not. A start-up mindset isn't about spreadsheets and SWOT analysis. It's about taking small, smart steps, being resourceful, and learning as you go. Most start-ups don't launch with a fully polished product. They start with the simplest version of an idea that can be tested and improved. Creatives can do the same. Instead of a novel, write a short story. Instead of a feature film, shoot a scene. Instead of a full album, release a single. The goal isn't perfection—it's momentum.

Get something out into the world, see how it resonates, and refine from there.

I have learned that, when I produce a movie, the finished film will never be as perfect as its promise, nor will it ever be as bad as it seems when looking at the first assembly. Your creative projects work the same way. It is a process of continuous iterative approach to a goal.

Ask yourself: What's the smallest version of this idea I can finish now? Do that. Then build from there.

Not everything I try works. That feels discouraging.

That's normal. In the start-up world, when something doesn't go as planned, the leaders pivot—adjusting course instead of clinging to a failing plan. If a project isn't landing, shift your approach. If an audience isn't responding, try a different angle. If you're hitting a wall, step back and reassess.

Isn't pivoting just a fancy word for quitting?

No. Quitting is stopping. Pivoting is adapting. You're finding a way to make it work. The best creatives aren't the ones who never fail. They're the ones who adjust, experiment, and keep moving forward.

Creatives often fear feedback, but successful start-ups thrive on it. They don't perfect a product in isolation; they test, listen, and refine. Share your work before you think it's ready. Ask specific questions. What works? What doesn't? What stands out? Then listen. Don't react defensively. Feedback isn't an attack—it's a tool. This ethos has even migrated to tech. At Google, they apply the "Beyoncé Rule," reworking a line from her song "Single Ladies": They say, "If you liked it, you shoulda put a test in it."

What if I get criticism I don't agree with?

That's okay. Not all feedback is useful. The key is to look for patterns. If multiple people say something isn't working, pay attention. If one person nitpicks something subjective, trust your instincts.

Most start-ups don't start with huge budgets. Neither do most creatives. But constraints are a gift. They force innovation. No expensive gear? Use what you have. No big network? Collaborate with peers. No time? Carve out small moments—consistency beats intensity. Free and low-cost tools exist for almost every creative field, and if you're resourceful, you can accomplish more than you think.

I feel like I never have enough—money, time, connections...

No one starts with "enough." The secret is to use what you've got and start anyway.

Branding isn't just for corporations. Your brand is simply how people understand your work. What's unique about what you create? What do you want people to feel when they experience it? What story are you telling, not just through your art, but about you? The clearer your message, the easier it is for the right audience to find and connect with your work.

But what if I just want to make things?

That's fine. But even if you don't think about branding, people will form an impression of you and your work anyway. You might as well have a say in what that impression is. Make it easier for the right people to find you. Start simple. Share your work with insight into your process. Engage with those who respond. Let it evolve as you grow.

Zooming out, your entire creative career is a start-up. Be strategic. Be intentional. Set goals: for the next project, for the next year, the next five years. Don't wait for the perfect opportunity. Create, release, learn, improve. Stay adaptable. If something isn't working, pivot, don't quit.

The biggest mistake creatives make is waiting for everything to be perfect before they begin. Start now, start small, and keep going.

Okay. My creative work is a start-up. I get it. What other business concepts do I need to know?

42

INTELLECTUAL PROPERTY AND COPYRIGHT

Your creative work isn't just an expression of your imagination—it's your intellectual property. That phrase might sound like it belongs in a lawyer's office, but it's something every creative person needs to understand. Your work has value. I'm talking money value: legal and financial. If you don't protect it, someone else might use it. Or worse, claim it as their own.

I always assumed my work was automatically protected. Do I really need to do anything?

Yes and no. Copyright protection kicks in the moment you create something original and fix it in a tangible form—write it down, record it, paint it. But understanding how copyright works and actively protecting your creations will give you the power to control your work's future.

Think of copyright as your creative shield. It applies to anything original that exists in a tangible medium. A manuscript saved on your computer is protected, but an idea for a book isn't. A painting on canvas has copyright protection, but the concept of a painting doesn't. A recorded song is copyrighted, but the melody you hum in the shower isn't—until you record it. Copyright gives you exclusive rights to reproduce, distribute, and adapt your work. In most cases, it lasts for your lifetime plus seventy years.

One simple way to reinforce your ownership is to include a copyright notice, like this:

Copyright © [Your Name] [Year]

That notice is not legally required, but it serves as a deterrent to others and makes your claim clear.

There is one more important step to take: Register your work with the Copyright Office. If someone tries to steal or misuse your work, a registered copyright makes enforcement easier.

But if copyright is automatic, why would I need to register it?

Registration strengthens your legal position. Without it, proving ownership can be difficult. With it, you have legal proof that the work is yours, and you can seek damages if necessary.

Registering is simple and inexpensive. You submit an online application to the US Copyright Office (or your country's equivalent), upload a copy of your work, pay a small fee, and receive a certificate confirming your ownership. If your work is ever stolen, this certificate is your best weapon.

What else can I do to protect my work?

Be proactive. Keep drafts, time stamps, and email records of your work's development—these provide evidence of authorship. Monitor where your work appears online. If you share your work digitally, use watermarks, upload low-resolution images, or license it through Creative Commons if you want control over how others use it.

Know the difference between *infringement* and *fair use*. Someone using a small portion of your work for commentary, criticism, or education may be protected under fair use, but wholesale copying is not. If you find your work being used without permission, act quickly. You can file a DMCA takedown notice for online violations or consult an attorney for serious cases.

This all feels overwhelming. Do I really need to worry about it now?

Not all at once. But at the very least, be aware of your rights. Add copyright notices to your work. Register the pieces that matter most. And pay attention to how your work is being shared. Protecting your creative work ensures that *you* benefit from its value, not someone else.

But copyright isn't just about defense—it's about empowerment. Knowing your rights gives you leverage in negotiations, licensing deals, and publishing agreements. It puts you in control.

"Leverage, negotiations, deals." This is feeling really business-y. Do I have to go that far?

43

CREATIVE LIFE AS BUSINESS OR HOBBY

Creativity is a powerful force, but how you choose to structure it in your life—whether as your livelihood or as a personal refuge—is entirely up to you. This decision shapes your work as well as your routines, priorities, and identity. Will you build a career around your creativity, or will you protect it from commercial pressures and keep it as a source of personal fulfillment? Neither path is superior. Both offer unique challenges and rewards. The key is to decide with intention, aligning your creative pursuits with your goals, financial needs, and personal values.

I always assumed if I was serious about my work, I had to make it my career. But is that really true?

You have options. Some of the greatest creative minds never made their art their primary source of income, while others thrived by dedicating their full professional lives to it. The important thing is understanding which approach fits you.

If you treat your creative work as a business, you're committing to making it financially sustainable. That means setting goals, managing deadlines, engaging with an audience, and adapting to market demands. It's rewarding, but it's also demanding. Monetizing your passion can shift your relationship with it. What once felt like pure expression might start feeling like work.

If you treat creativity as a hobby, it remains a sanctuary—free from financial pressure, deadlines, and expectations. You can explore and experiment on your own terms, but without external structure, it may be harder to stay disciplined or motivated to grow.

Does that mean I have to choose one forever?

There is no forever. Many creatives move between these approaches depending on their circumstances. Wallace Stevens was a Pulitzer Prize-winning poet, yet he never left his job as an insurance executive. His poetry wasn't less meaningful because it wasn't his livelihood. Maya Angelou worked a range of jobs—streetcar conductor, dancer, journalist—before her writing career took off. Those experiences fueled her art, proving that a creative career doesn't have to follow a straight path.

Terry Crews, best known as an actor and former football player, is also an accomplished painter. His artwork isn't his primary income, but it remains a vital creative outlet that fuels his overall artistic expression. He doesn't rely on it to pay the bills, and that freedom allows him to create for the pure joy of it.

So how do I decide which path is right for me?

Start by considering your financial reality. If you need a steady income, keeping creativity as a side pursuit while you build skills and an audience might be the best option. If you have financial flexibility, transitioning into a full-time creative career might be viable.

Ask yourself if you enjoy the business side of creativity. Running a creative business means more than making art—it involves marketing, networking, and financial management. Some people thrive in that environment; others find it drains their passion.

Consider your relationship with risk and uncertainty. A creative career often involves inconsistent income and unpredictable opportunities. Some people thrive in that uncertainty; others find it stressful. Be honest about your tolerance for financial instability.

Most importantly, ask yourself what brings you joy. Some people love turning their passion into a profession; others find that monetization strips away the love they once had for their work. You need to determine what aligns with your personality and goals.

What if I make the wrong choice?

You won't. Because this choice isn't permanent. You can shift over time. Many creatives start as hobbyists and turn professional. Others scale back from professional work to rediscover their creative joy. The key is flexibility—allowing yourself to adapt as your circumstances and desires change.

Okay, if I want to turn creativity into my career, where do I start?

44

EMPLOYMENT VS. GIG ECONOMICS

Your creative career will likely swing between two worlds: traditional employment and gig work. In the first, they give you a 401(k); in the second, you make your own. Each offers different opportunities and challenges, and learning to navigate both is key to sustaining both your creative life and financial stability. Whether you thrive in the structure of a steady paycheck or the flexibility of freelancing, understanding these dynamics will help you make informed choices.

I feel like I should be all-in on one or the other, but I don't know which is right for me.

You don't have to choose just one forever. Most creatives move between traditional jobs and freelance work depending on their needs, projects, and financial situation. Each has its place, and that's been my career path. A traditional job provides stability—predictable income, benefits like health insurance and retirement plans, and a clear professional path. But it can also come with creative restrictions, fixed hours, and limited freedom to choose your projects.

Freelance or gig work, on the other hand, gives you autonomy. You pick the projects, set your own schedule, and follow your creative instincts without answering to a boss. But that freedom comes with uncertainty. You have to manage your own income, handle inconsistent paychecks, and navigate taxes, contracts, and client relationships on your own.

So which one is better?

It depends on your goals and circumstances. Some creatives thrive in a structured job that provides financial security while they develop their personal projects on the side. Others feel stifled by traditional employment and need the flexibility of gig work to keep their creativity alive. The real key is learning to move between these worlds strategically.

But what if I want both? Is that possible?

Absolutely. Many successful creatives blend both paths. Phoebe Waller-Bridge, before creating *Fleabag*, balanced traditional acting roles with freelance writing. The financial stability of employment gave her the freedom to develop the independent work that ultimately launched her global success. Questlove, the bandleader for *The Tonight Show*, treats that role as his "day job" while pursuing side gigs as a producer, DJ, and author. His steady employment provides security, while his freelance projects fuel his creativity. Greta Gerwig worked between salaried acting jobs and gig-based writing and directing, using each to refine her path as a filmmaker.

You can use full-time employment to build savings and develop skills, which in turn support your freelance career. Likewise, you can use gig work to explore creative interests and gain experience that makes you more competitive for traditional roles.

How do I know when to switch between them?

Look at your financial and creative needs. If stability is your priority—if you need health insurance, consistent paychecks, or a structured schedule—a traditional job may be the right choice for now. If you're in a period of creative growth, seeking independence, or willing to take financial risks, gig work might be a better fit.

Timing also matters. You might take on a day job to save money before launching an independent project. Or you might lean into gig work during a life transition, when flexibility is more valuable than stability.

That makes sense, but I feel overwhelmed by the financial side of all this.

That's normal. Creatives often struggle with financial planning because income fluctuates, especially in gig work. If you're in a traditional job, maximize employer benefits—contribute to retirement plans, take advantage of health insurance, and set aside money for future projects. If you're freelancing, plan for income variability. Save aggressively during high-earning periods so you can sustain yourself during slower months. Retirement planning is still possible with gig work—options like SEP IRAs or Solo 401(k)s allow you to invest in your future even without an employer.

What about the emotional side? Freelancing sounds freeing, but also kind of lonely.

It can be. Traditional employment gives you colleagues, mentorship, and a built-in support system. Freelancing requires more effort to maintain a sense of community. Find other creatives who are on a similar path, whether through online forums, local groups, or industry events. Staying connected helps prevent isolation and keeps you in the loop for new opportunities.

It sounds like both paths have trade-offs. How do I make the most of whichever one I choose?

If you're in a traditional job, protect your personal creative time. Block off hours for your own projects so your creative work doesn't get lost in the routine of a paycheck. Use your job's stability to invest in yourself—whether that's saving money, learning new skills, or expanding your professional network.

If you're freelancing, build a financial safety net. Budget wisely, take on a mix of projects, and diversify your income streams so you're not dependent on a single client. Invest in tools, education, and professional development to stay competitive.

Regardless of which path you're on, relationships matter. Build a network that spans both traditional and freelance spaces. People you work with today might open doors for you down the road—whether it's a full-time job or an unexpected collaboration.

So I don't have to pick one forever?

You won't. Your creative career will shift between employment and gig work, sometimes by necessity, sometimes by choice. The key is to be intentional, knowing when to lean into structure and when to embrace independence. One fuels the other. Stability gives freedom; freedom opens doors to stability.

I want to be there. But I have to pay the rent.

45

THE DAY JOB

Your creative work deserves to thrive, but for many, a day job provides the foundation that makes that possible. Whether it's paying the bills, building connections, or serving as a stepping-stone, a day job can be your greatest ally in sustaining your creative pursuits—if you approach it with intention and strategy.

I worry that having a day job means I'm not a real artist. Shouldn't I be all in?

You can still be all in. A day job offers something invaluable: stability. Financial security takes away the persistent anxiety of making ends meet, leaving you the mental space to focus on your craft. T.S. Eliot worked as a banker while writing *The Waste Land*, one of the most transformative poems of the twentieth century. His steady income gave him the freedom to write without compromise.

Your day job can also be a surprising source of inspiration. Charles Bukowski's years at the post office gave him material for his gritty, unfiltered poetry. Before she became a punk rock icon, Patti Smith worked in factories and at a bookstore. Yes, she had to pay the bills; she also enriched her creative perspective. And beyond inspiration, day jobs teach discipline. Juggling work and creativity forces you to make every hour count. The difference between someone who dreams of creating and someone who actually creates often comes down to how they manage their time.

But what if my day job drains me?

That's the risk. If a day job is too demanding, it can leave you too exhausted to create, turning the thing you love into a neglected corner of your life. Time constraints can push your creative goals to "someday," and if your work feels disconnected from your artistic identity, it may begin to chip away at your sense of purpose. This is why it's so important to approach your day job strategically, making sure it works for you, not against you.

How do I make sure my day job supports my creative life instead of suffocating it?

Start by choosing the right kind of work. A job that complements your creativity—whether through flexibility, low stress, or direct relevance to your craft—will make a huge difference. Teaching art, working in a library, or taking a part-time administrative role in a creative organization are great options. If that's not possible, then setting clear boundaries becomes essential. Your day job is not your life. Learn to say "no" to extra responsibilities or overtime that encroaches on your creative time.

Scheduling creative time is just as important as any work meeting. Viola Davis didn't win an Academy Award by accident. Between day jobs, she carved out disciplined time for acting. She treated her craft as nonnegotiable, making space for it no matter what else was going on. You can do the same. Use a calendar or an alarm—whatever it takes to signal to yourself and others that this is your time to create.

I don't want my day job to feel like a waste of time. Is there a way to use it creatively?

Absolutely. Pay attention to the people, dynamics, and stories around you. Philip Glass drove a taxi for years in New York City, while in his off time he worked on his musical compositions that would revolutionize minimalism. He found inspiration working on mundane tasks. Maybe you can hear the repetitions of daily life in his music. Your day job, even if it's not glamorous, can be a wellspring of material if you approach it with that mindset. Keep a notebook, set down observations, ideas, or snippets of conversation that may spark something later.

Creativity also needs energy. If your day job takes all of yours, you won't have much left for your art. Prioritize rest, nutrition, and recovery. A short walk after work, a breathing exercise, or even a five-minute stretch can reset your focus. The goal isn't just to carve out time for creativity, but to show up for it with energy and clarity.

But I don't want to be stuck in a day job forever.

You don't have to be. Many creatives use their day jobs as a stepping-stone. T.S. Eliot didn't stay a banker forever. Charles Bukowski eventually left the post office, but only after years of writing every night. Greta Gerwig moved between salaried acting jobs and freelance directing gigs, using each to fund and shape her creative path. Having a day job doesn't mean giving up—it means supporting yourself while you build something real.

What if I start to resent my day job?

Check in with yourself regularly. Is your day job still supporting your goals? If it's draining you more than it's helping, it might be time to pivot. Can you switch to part time? Can you freelance? Can you move to a role that's more creatively fulfilling? Yes, some jobs can be prisons, and those are the jobs you don't want; you want the job that is freedom.

Treat your day job as part of your creative ecosystem. By choosing wisely, protecting your time, and staying disciplined, you can make sure your day job pays the bills while leaving room for your craft to flourish. Your creativity is worth the effort it takes to find that balance. And who knows? Like Patti Smith or Philip Glass, the time spent at your day job may end up fueling your most profound creations.

I'll work on that balance. But I'm not making any money from my creative work.

46

IF YOU WANT TO EARN MONEY, YOU NEED A PRODUCT TO SELL

What can I buy from you right now?

Huh?

Creativity alone isn't enough to make a living. You need something tangible, something people can buy, engage with, or support. This is where many creatives hesitate, caught in the gap between artistic expression and market reality. But the truth is, your creative product is more than just a transaction. It's a way to share your work with the world, connect with your audience, and ensure your creativity has a sustainable foundation.

Your creativity is your gift, but your product is what brings that gift into the world. Even the most talented artist, writer, or musician will struggle to gain traction without something to offer. A product serves as the physical or digital representation of your work, a way for others to connect with it—and with you.

Think of it this way: Your product is the bridge between your inner creative world and the people waiting to support you. It doesn't have to be perfect; it just has to exist. Without it, your creativity remains a private endeavor, hidden from the world.

But what if I don't have anything to sell?

Start by looking at what you already have. Your first product is likely hiding in plain sight. Writers might compile existing essays into an eBook. Musicians could release a few recorded tracks as a mini album. Visual artists might create prints of their work.

You don't need to launch with a grand, perfected vision. Start small. A minimum viable product— an "MVP" in business-speak, a single, testable offering—will help you gauge interest and build confidence. Instead of overthinking or waiting for perfection, focus on getting something tangible into the hands of your audience.

I don't even know where to begin. What kind of product makes sense for me?

It depends on your medium. Digital products like ebooks, downloadable art, or music tracks are low-cost to produce. Physical goods—prints, handcrafted items, signed editions—create a sense of exclusivity. Experiences like workshops, live performances, or personalized lessons turn your skills into something people can engage with. Even licensing your work—selling music for commercials or illustrations for book covers—can be a powerful revenue stream. The key is to find what feels natural to you and start there.

That sounds great in theory, but what if no one buys it?

That's the fear that holds so many creatives back. What if no one cares? What if people criticize it? What if it's not good enough?

Here's the truth: Putting your work out there is always a vulnerable act, but it's also a powerful one. Reframe selling as an act of generosity. You're not forcing anything on anyone. You're offering your art to people who want to support it.

Start with a small, safe audience. Offer your product to friends, family, or an online community where you already have connections. This builds confidence and gives you a soft launch before reaching wider audiences. And separate yourself from your work, because your product is not your identity. Feedback, whether good or bad, is just information to help you grow.

Has anyone actually built a career this way?

Rupi Kaur started with self-publishing. She didn't wait for perfection—she compiled poems she'd already written, designed a simple cover, and promoted *Milk and Honey* through Instagram. That willingness to treat her work as a product allowed her to reach millions.

Andy Weir's *The Martian* began as free chapters posted online. When readers clamored for more, he self-published it as an ebook priced at ninety-nine cents. The book became a bestseller and later a hit movie. Because he took that first step.

Amanda Palmer built an entire career by understanding the power of connection. She offers music downloads, personalized merchandise, and exclusive content, using platforms like Kickstarter and Patreon to engage directly with her audience. Her dedicated fanbase doesn't just buy her work—they invest in her vision.

Okay, I'm convinced. But how do I actually make this happen?

Start by packaging your work professionally. Even the simplest product should look polished. If you're designing an ebook or an album cover, online tools can help, or you can hire a freelancer and support the circular creative economy. And choose the right platform for selling, where customers will logically look for work like yours.

Pricing can feel tricky, but the key is to find a balance, something accessible but reflective of your effort. Research similar products to find a fair price point. And when it comes time to promote, don't let fear hold you back. Share the story behind your work. Let people into your process. Connection sells more than perfection.

But what if it doesn't sell? What if I put in all this work and no one buys it?

Then you learn. Your first product will be a stepping-stone. Treat it as an experiment. Gather feedback, refine, and improve for next time. No one gets it perfect the first time. What matters is that you start.

Your first product is a milestone. It's the beginning of financial sustainability, but more than that, it's the moment when your creativity stops being theoretical and becomes something real.

The idea I have feels perfect, transformative even. But how do I know if anyone will actually pay for it?

47

HOW TO TEST IF YOUR PROJECT MAY BE COMMERCIAL BEFORE YOU GO TOO DEEP

Many creatives avoid asking themselves if an audience will buy their product because they are worried this question will kill their creativity. Testing doesn't kill creativity; it channels it toward an audience that's ready for it. The world is full of brilliant ideas that never found their place, not because they weren't good, but because their creators didn't stop to check if anyone was waiting for them.

Market-testing is a way of bridging instinct with reality. It's how you figure out if your idea resonates, if it's viable, and if it needs adjustment before you invest months or years into it. You're gathering data to make your work stronger.

But doesn't that take all the magic out of it?

Testing does not change your vision. It is about making sure your vision lands with your audience. Is your meaning clear? How should you position your work so people will engage with it? The goal isn't to make something for everyone. It's to find the audience that's already hungry for what you're creating.

Start by defining your audience. Who will love this? Who needs this? Picture the person who will be first in line to buy it. Then figure out if there are enough of them to sustain what you're building. Look at similar projects. How have they performed? What worked? What didn't? You can map the landscape before you step into it.

What if there's nothing else like my idea?

That's unlikely, and that's a good thing. A completely untested market means you'll have to build awareness from scratch, which is expensive and exhausting. The better play is to find comparables, creative works that share elements with your idea but aren't exactly the same. If you're writing a novel, check Goodreads or Amazon reviews for books in a similar genre. If you're launching an indie film, study what audiences responded to. If you're selling a handmade product, explore Etsy trends to see what's getting traction.

I'm nervous about sharing my idea before it's ready.

That fear is normal, but it's also what keeps too many creatives stuck in their own heads. Testing doesn't mean exposing your roughest draft to the whole world. Start small. Share concept sketches, a sample chapter, or a teaser clip in a controlled environment—an online community, a Discord group, or even a private mailing list. Watch the responses. Do people light up? Do they ask when they can get more?

Even though they have been somewhat overused, crowdfunding platforms remain some of the best ways to test demand. They don't just provide funding; they give real-world proof that people want what you're making. Email sign-ups, pre-orders, and engagement metrics can also be strong indicators. If your idea doesn't get traction early, that's essential feedback. You now have data to use to tweak, reposition, or rethink your idea before going all in.

But what if people don't like it?

Then you learn. That's the point. If your idea isn't landing, you can refine it, shift your approach, or pivot entirely. Testing before you go deep saves you from investing in something that was never going to work.

The most successful creatives aren't just visionaries; they're adaptable. They find the people who want what they're making and give it to them in a way that resonates.

Okay. I get that I need to sell something. But how do I do that?

48

THERE ARE ONLY FOUR WAYS TO MONETIZE YOUR CREATIVE WORK

No matter how innovative things seem, every way to make money from creative work falls into one of four models: for sale, for rent, on subscription, or free (advertising-supported). Richard Abramowitz, who distributed more documentaries than anyone on the planet, taught me this principle.

That can't be right. What about streaming? NFTs? Crowdfunding?

They all fit within these models. Whether you're selling an ancient epic, renting a medieval manuscript, or streaming a video today, the structure remains the same. The tools and technology evolve, but the fundamental ways creative work is monetized never change.

Selling is the most straightforward. You create something, and someone buys it. Writers sell books. Filmmakers sell movies to distributors. Digital artists sell NFTs. If you've ever listed your work on Etsy or Shopify you're part of this tradition. It offers an immediate exchange—make something, get paid—but also requires a steady stream of new buyers or new work.

Renting gives people temporary access without ownership. Musicians license songs for commercials. Playwrights license their plays for performance. Photographers rent out images for editorial use. Digital artists lease animations for brand campaigns. Actors and singers in effect rent their time for rehearsals and performances; then the venue lets you rent your seat for a few hours during the play or concert. This model allows a single piece of work to generate income multiple times.

Subscriptions create recurring income. Charles Dickens serialized *The Pickwick Papers*, selling each installment to subscribers who paid in advance. Today, Patreon, Substack, and YouTube memberships operate on the same principle: ongoing payments in exchange for continuous content. This model builds a direct relationship between creators and audiences, ensuring steady support rather than one-time sales.

Advertising-supported work flips the equation: Instead of asking the audience to pay, you let brands or sponsors foot the bill. Advertiser-supported YouTube, TikTok, and podcasts operate this way, just as early newspapers relied on merchant ads to fund printing costs. This model works best at scale—when you have a large enough audience, advertisers will pay for access to them.

Most successful creatives don't rely on just one model, they mix them. A musician might sell albums, license songs for commercials, release bonus tracks on Patreon, and post free music videos on YouTube monetized through ads. A filmmaker might sell a film to distributors, license clips for use in documentaries, offer behind-the-scenes content to subscribers, and release trailers for free on social media. Each model supports the others, creating a sustainable creative career.

So, how do I know which one is right for me?

Start by asking yourself what kind of relationship you want with your audience. If you want them to own your work outright, selling might be the best approach. If they only need temporary access, renting could make sense. If you can produce a steady stream of content, subscriptions might be the right fit. If your goal is mass reach, offering free content supported by advertising could help you grow.

No single model is better than the others. You need to find what aligns with your work and your audience. You can always adapt. What starts as a rental could evolve into a sale. What begins as free might lead to a successful subscription.

Beeple, the digital artist, sold an NFT for $69 million. Amanda Palmer built a career on Patreon. MrBeast posts free videos so he can earn millions from ads and sponsors. Taylor Swift sells albums, licenses music for commercials, and streams on Spotify. They didn't invent new ways to monetize—they mastered existing ones.

Every successful creative, from the earliest storytellers to today's biggest influencers, has worked within these four models. You just need to decide where your work fits.

Then you have to tell people about it.

I just want to focus on my work. Do I have to deal with social media?

49

MEDIA (SOCIAL AND OTHERWISE) IS PART OF YOUR SETUP

When you're done with your work, you're only half-done. Now you have to make sure people know about it. If a tree falls in the forest…, you know?

Whether you're writing a novel, producing a film, or designing a collection, your audience won't find you by accident. Media—especially social media—is the bridge between your art and the world. It's no longer optional; it's a tool you must wield effectively to connect, build, and sustain your audience. And the time to start isn't when your project is complete. The time to start is now.

But isn't social media just self-promotion?

Social media is about connection. And your business. Because distributors, anyone who will take your work the last mile to its audience, expect you to bring your audience with you and deliver it to the distributor all packaged and ready. In the past, creatives relied on publishers, galleries, or agencies to amplify their work. Today, you have direct access to your audience through platforms like Instagram, TikTok, and LinkedIn. This access is powerful, and you will be expected to leverage it, so it requires intention and strategy.

Social media lets you build anticipation. When you share the story of your process, people become invested. They will be interested in more than your single, temporal work: They will be interested in you. Connection turns casual scrollers into dedicated supporters. First provide value, then ask. Share your inspirations, behind-the-scenes progress, and the highs and lows of creation. By the time you're ready to launch, your audience won't just be interested. They'll be cheering you on.

Okay, but where do I even start?

Think of your media presence as storytelling. Define your goals. What do you want your audience to feel, know, or do? Who is your ideal audience? Are you speaking to fans, collaborators, or potential clients? Write it down: "My audience is [describe them], and I want them to [desired action]." This clarity will guide everything you post.

Focus your energy where it counts. You don't need to be everywhere—just on the social platforms where your audience is. Plan your content rather than posting randomly. Think about the story you're telling. Show the messy sketches as well as the polished work. Share the days you're inspired and the ones you're not. Use a comprehensive social media app to create and schedule posts in advance, so you're not scrambling every day.

Isn't it too soon to start sharing if I don't have a finished project?

Start now. Start before you think you're ready. Share the beginnings, the research, the drafts, the ideas. It might feel premature, but it's not. When Devon Rodriguez, the New York street portrait artist, was starting his career, he posted portrait sketches on TikTok; the feedback from that community helped him refine his style and propelled him to virality.

Consistency is key. Whether you post once a day or once a week, do it regularly. A predictable rhythm builds trust with your audience, even if it's just a single post every Sunday. And don't just broadcast—engage.

Ask your followers questions, run polls, or let them weigh in on creative choices. People love to feel included.

But I don't want to turn into an influencer.

You don't have to. You just have to be visible enough to let people discover your work. Bo Burnham didn't wait for permission to perform; he shared his comedic songs on YouTube, where they found an immediate audience. Many writers and musicians use Patreon to connect with fans directly, offering them behind-the-scenes updates and personal insights.

Treat your supporters as collaborators in your journey. Even if your style isn't as public-facing as some of the people I've mentioned, the lesson is clear: Your audience wants to feel like they're part of your story. When you share authentically, you turn them into advocates for your work.

This all sounds like a lot. How do I make it manageable?

It doesn't have to take over your life. Batch your content. Spend an afternoon each month planning posts, then schedule them with applications made for that purpose. Use analytics tools to track what resonates and adjust your content accordingly. Emphasize engagement over perfection. Spontaneous videos or candid updates often perform better than polished content. Reply to comments and answer questions. These small gestures build loyalty. Set aside fifteen minutes a day to connect. Show, don't just tell. Visuals, videos, and behind-the-scenes glimpses make your posts dynamic. Let your audience see the process; then they will discover the product.

Your media presence is both a megaphone and part of your creative toolkit. It's how you build relationships, share your journey, and lay the groundwork for your next big project. Think of it as part of your setup, just like choosing your materials or finding your collaborators. When done thoughtfully, it becomes a seamless extension of your art.

I don't know… I still feel weird about putting myself out there.

Then start small. Share something that feels safe, a quote that inspires you, a behind-the-scenes snapshot, a work in progress. Then post a bit more. Listen to the feedback. Give gratitude. By the time your project is ready, your audience will already be there, ready to celebrate with you.

And now, with your media setup in place, it's time to get practical. You need to make a budget for your projects, plus the time, tools, and resources that make your creative life sustainable.

I'm not very good with money.

50

MAKE A REALISTIC BUDGET

Budgeting is a learned skill. No one came out of the womb knowing anything about money. But if you don't find a way to be in control of money, your work won't get made. Or worse, it'll get made, and then you'll realize you can't afford to finish or share it. Every creative project starts with a spark of inspiration, but turning that inspiration into something more concrete requires a budget.

Think of your budget as a road map. It guides your project from idea to completion, showing you where your resources need to go and ensuring you don't lose your way. Budgeting is about aligning your ambitions with what's achievable. A good budget is a source of freedom. It lets you focus on your creativity without constantly worrying about where the money will come from.

But what if I don't know how to budget?

You start by making it realistic. That means basing it on actual costs, matching it to the scope of your project, and being honest about what you can afford. But realistic doesn't mean rigid; a good budget also has room to adapt when things don't go exactly as planned. And trust me, they won't. The good news? A well-prepared budget will help you handle surprises without derailing your entire project.

What do you mean by a "realistic" budget?

Realistic means grounded in research, aligned with the size of your project, and achievable within your resources. If you're shooting a short film, don't aim for Hollywood-level production. Instead, focus on what you can do brilliantly within your limits. A realistic budget also has flexibility, because unexpected expenses will pop up, and you need to be ready for them.

Start by listing everything your project needs. Do your research. Call venues for rental costs, check prices for supplies, and ask peers what they've spent on similar projects. It might take time, but every dollar you plan for now saves you five dollars of panic later. And always add a contingency fund—a common contingency is 5 to 10 percent of your total budget—to cover surprises. Think of it as your safety net.

This sounds overwhelming. Have people really made great work on small budgets?

Absolutely. Robert Rodriguez shot *El Mariachi* for just $7,000 by doing everything himself—directing, editing, even handling sound design. He borrowed equipment, used friends as actors, and worked within his means. He showed me the receipts. When I was at Disney I flew him from Texas for his first trip to Hollywood. His story is proof that creativity flourishes within constraints.

Ava DuVernay, before her rise as a major filmmaker, made her early films with micro-budgets, relying on familiar locations and intimate storytelling to keep costs low. Even Margaret Atwood self-published some of her poetry early in her career, carefully managing every expense and learning the value of tracking her finances.

What these stories show is that resourcefulness is just as important as money. A limited budget means you need to prioritize and plan.

How do I actually build a budget?

Break your budget into clear categories: personnel costs, materials, equipment, location fees, marketing, distribution, administrative expenses, and a contingency fund. Assign an estimated cost to each one to stay organized.

Be honest about what matters most. If something doesn't directly contribute to your project's success, consider cutting it. A budget is a plan. Add a contingency fund, because no matter how well you prepare, something unexpected will always come up.

What if I go over budget?

Budgeting doesn't stop once the numbers are written down. Track every expense in real time. Use apps, spreadsheets, or just a notebook to monitor spending and make adjustments if you're veering off course. Be smart about where you spend. Shop secondhand, barter services, or borrow equipment whenever possible. Communicate with your team so everyone understands the financial boundaries.

Your budget is the foundation of your creative project. With a realistic budget, you can focus on making your work the best it can be, free from the stress of unplanned costs or financial uncertainty. A budget gives your creativity room to thrive.

Okay, I can see the value in this. But how do I budget my own time? I don't just need money; I need to protect my hours so I can actually get the work done.

51

CHARGE FOR YOUR TIME

Many of us were raised on the erroneous belief-system that creativity should flow freely, unencumbered by the mundane concerns of money. Let's reframe: Charging for your time isn't just about earning a living. It's about respecting yourself and the value of your time.

Value my hours? I don't know what to charge.

That's because you haven't fully accepted that your time has value.

This simple truth may be one of the hardest for creatives to embrace. Whether you're designing, writing, performing, or creating something entirely unique, the time and expertise you bring to your craft are valuable. And the sooner you own that truth, the sooner others will, too.

I get it, but what if people don't want to pay?

Time is the one resource you can never get back. Every hour spent on creative work—sketching a concept, refining a manuscript, rehearsing a performance—is time you could be spending elsewhere. Charging for it ensures that you're compensated for your effort and also for the opportunity cost of not doing something else.

More than that, charging for your time signals professionalism. When you confidently set rates and stick to them, clients and collaborators recognize that you take your work, and theirs, seriously. It also sustains your creativity. Income from your time allows you to invest in better tools, more learning opportunities, and ultimately, more time to create.

I know I should charge, but asking for money feels weird.

That's because creatives are often conditioned to feel guilty about it. You might worry that your work isn't "worth it" or fear rejection if your rates seem too high. But here's the truth: Your skills, talent, and time are valuable, and people who appreciate quality will pay for them.

Try this exercise: Write down ten ways your work benefits others. Maybe your designs help businesses attract clients, or your music provides solace and joy. Seeing this list can build confidence in the value you offer. Then, practice saying your rates out loud: "My rate for this project is $150/hour." Say it again. And again. Repeating it helps you own it emotionally and makes it easier to communicate.

How do I even decide what to charge?

There are several ways to price your work. An hourly rate is the simplest—calculate what you need to earn monthly, divide it by your available working hours, and add a margin for savings and profit. If a project is more about results than time spent, charge a flat project fee instead. Retainer agreements provide a steady income for ongoing work, while value-based pricing aligns your fee with the impact of what you create. Some creatives even use a subscription model, offering exclusive content or mentorship for a recurring fee.

Is this really how successful creatives operate?

Absolutely. Andy Warhol didn't just charge for paintings. He charged for his time, his brand, and his influence. Shonda Rhimes, who creates high-profile TV shows, negotiates deals based on the value of her ideas and the revenue they would generate. Even Banksy, despite his anti-establishment persona, understands that pricing his work allows him to control his art and his narrative.

Okay, but I'm just getting started. Should I charge less?

It's fine to start small, but don't undervalue yourself. Research industry rates, be up front about pricing, and never work for "exposure" unless it's on your own terms. If a client pushes back on your rates, consider adjusting scope, not price. And if someone truly doesn't respect your value, don't be afraid to walk away.

I think I understand. It's about valuing myself.

Exactly. Charging for your time is one of the most empowering steps you can take as a creative. You are standing up for the value of your work. Your skills. Yourself.

How will I know how long my projects will take?

52

KNOW HOW MUCH TIME IT TAKES

One of the most common mistakes creatives make is underestimating time. You advance your art when you manage expectations, price your work accurately, and respect your own time. If you don't know how much time your creative work takes, you can't value it properly. And that affects everything: your income, your reputation, and your sanity.

I never know how long something will take until I'm already behind.

Think of your time as a currency. Every hour you spend on a project is an investment, and like any smart investor, you need to know how much you're putting in and what kind of return you can expect. If you don't, you risk undercharging, overpromising, and, ultimately, burning out.

Accurate time estimates allow you to set realistic prices. If you're charging hourly, you need to know how many hours to bill. If you're charging per project, knowing how long it will take ensures your rate is fair. This is professionalism. When you can confidently provide clients with realistic timelines and stick to them, you build trust. And trust is the foundation of every successful creative career.

I just guess—and I'm always wrong.

That's because you're thinking in broad strokes instead of breaking your project into smaller, more manageable pieces. Let's say you're designing a logo. Instead of thinking, "This will take me about two weeks," break it down. How long will you spend researching? Sketching concepts? Revising based on client feedback? Each step gets its own time estimate, which you can then add up.

Next, look at past projects. Think about similar work you've done: How long did it take? What challenges came up? If you're not sure, start keeping a time log for your current projects.

And don't forget to factor in buffers. Creative work is rarely linear, and unexpected delays are common. Add an extra 20 to 30 percent to your estimate to account for revisions, distractions, and surprises. This contingency will protect you and your project from the unexpected. Other creatives in your field can offer invaluable insights into how long similar projects took them.

Then to schedule yourself, try reverse calendar planning. Start with your deadline and work backward, assigning specific blocks of time to each task.

Do successful creatives actually do this?

Yes. The best in the business know exactly how long their work takes.

Stephen King, one of the most prolific writers of our time, knows he can complete six pages a day, no more, no less. By sticking to this consistent output, he can estimate how long a novel will take with uncanny precision. His advice? "Amateurs sit and wait for inspiration, the rest of us just get up and go to work."

Maya Lin, the architect behind the Vietnam Veterans Memorial, is another expert of time management. She divides her projects into clear phases—research, design, execution—and creates detailed schedules for each. This disciplined approach allows her to balance creativity with practical deadlines, delivering work that's both inspired and on time.

Then there's Pixar. Their films take years to make, and every minute is accounted for. By meticulously tracking time spent on each phase—storyboarding, animation, revisions—they ensure realistic schedules without stifling creativity. It's a perfect example of how planning and artistry can coexist.

So if I don't know how long something takes, I should start tracking it now?

Exactly. Knowing how much time your creative work takes is one of the most empowering skills you can develop. It allows you to set fair prices, meet deadlines, and manage your workload with confidence. But more than that, it's a way to respect your craft and yourself.

Every project is a learning opportunity, so track your time, refine your estimates, and trust that you're getting better with each step.

Okay, I can track my time. But what about actually paying myself? I always put myself last.

53

PAY YOURSELF FIRST

I want to invest everything in my work. Isn't that what dedication looks like?

It's easy to believe that. The art, the music, the writing—those are the things that define you, right? But here's the truth: You are the center of it all. Without you, your creative projects don't happen. That's why paying yourself first isn't just a financial strategy; it's a profound act of valuing yourself. It says: "I matter. My time, energy, and stability matter."

Yet paying yourself first can feel counterintuitive. Creatives are often tempted to invest every dollar and every ounce of energy back into their work. They think: If I just finish this project, just buy this tool, just make this thing perfect, then it will all pay off.

But that cycle can leave you depleted, both financially and emotionally. Paying yourself first breaks that cycle. My friend, you gotta eat.

But isn't the work the most important thing?

You are the most important asset in your creative career. Can you embrace this? Your talent, your ideas, your ability to show up and do the work generates every dollar, every opportunity, every breakthrough. If you neglect yourself, everything else falls apart.

Paying yourself first ensures sustainability. If you're constantly pouring all your resources into your projects without reserving anything for yourself, you'll eventually run dry. You can't create from a place of exhaustion or financial insecurity. Paying yourself first is a way of saying, I need to be okay first, so I can keep going.

It also reflects your worth. If you don't value yourself, how can you expect anyone else to? Clients, collaborators, and audiences pick up on how you treat yourself. Prioritizing your needs sets a tone of professionalism and confidence that others respect.

Okay, but how do I actually do this?

Start by setting up a pay structure. Decide what percentage of your income will go to you personally before anything else. A good starting point is 20 percent, but you can adjust based on your circumstances. If a client pays you $1,000, you immediately set aside $200 for yourself before touching the rest.

Automate your savings. Have your bank automatically transfer a portion of your earnings into a savings or retirement account. This ensures you're building a financial cushion without having to think about it.

Build a buffer. Freelancing or gig work often comes with income fluctuations. So you also need to set aside some part of each payment into a rainy-day fund. This stability reduces stress and keeps you afloat during lean times.

Treat every project like a business deal. Dedicate a specific percentage of earnings to yourself as "profit." If a project earns $5,000, allocate half for personal pay and half for expenses and reinvestment.

It's not just about the immediate money?

There's more to it. Your time and energy are just as valuable. Protect your creative time. Before you commit to external projects or collaborations, block out hours in your week for your own creative growth. These are *nonnegotiable* hours, sacred time for experimenting, learning, or simply dreaming.

Prioritize self-care. Creativity thrives when you are well. Invest in practices that keep you energized and focused, like exercise, meditation, or therapy. These aren't indulgences; they're essential investments.

Celebrate small wins. Paying yourself isn't just about dollars. When you finish a project or hit a milestone, reward yourself. It could be as simple as a favorite meal, a day off, or a meaningful treat. These moments of joy keep you motivated.

Invest in your growth. Use part of your pay to develop your skills. Sign up for a workshop, buy that book on craft, or upgrade your tools. Every dollar you invest in yourself pays dividends in your creative future.

Do successful creatives actually do this?

Absolutely. Oprah Winfrey, early in her career, negotiated deals that reflected her worth. Her financial acumen gave her the freedom to take creative risks. She understood that paying herself first wasn't just smart—it was essential.

Elizabeth Gilbert worked odd jobs while setting aside time and money for her writing. Her commitment to paying herself first ensured she could keep creating, even when her books weren't yet bestsellers.

David Lynch carved out time for meditation and creative experiments before taking on paid work. By paying himself first spiritually and emotionally, he sustained decades of groundbreaking creativity.

So paying myself first actually makes my creative life more sustainable?

Exactly. Paying yourself first manufactures a sustainable future for your creativity. It's a way of respecting your work, your time, and your worth. When you prioritize yourself, you build toward your lasting success.

That makes sense. But how do I make sure I'm getting the best opportunities for my work?

54

BE YOUR OWN AGENT

Someone with connections and influence who champions your work, securing deals, and making your creative life effortless is a nice fantasy.

But, reality check: No one will ever care as much about your work as you do. And even if you land a dream agent, the bulk of your opportunities will still come from your own efforts.

Becoming your own agent isn't just a necessity; it's empowering. It puts you in control of your creative career. You learn to advocate for yourself, open doors, navigate opportunities. Best of all, it teaches you the skills that will serve you with or without an agent.

But aren't agents supposed to do this for me?

Agents, while valuable, aren't magical fixers. Many focus on their top-earning clients, and for creatives starting out, their hustle is often a lower priority. Good agents do care, but their resources are limited, and they need to focus where they see the greatest immediate return.

Even if you have an agent, the skills of pitching, networking, and negotiating remain critical for you. Think of yourself as your own front line.

I don't even know where to start.

Start by thinking about yourself in the way your buyer, the client who will hire you, might think about you. How will they look for you? Embed the way you want to be identified within your description of yourself, and define what makes your work unique and why it matters. Write a one-sentence pitch that captures your creative identity; for example, *I'm a digital artist who creates surreal landscapes that explore themes of identity and memory.* This pitch becomes your foundation, shaping how you talk about your work and present yourself professionally.

Build a portfolio that showcases your best work. Whether it's a website, a digital reel, or a social media showcase, make sure it's easy to navigate and clearly represents what you do. Make it polished and professional.

Networking, in my definition and practice of it, is making genuine connections. Ask questions, show interest in others, and be part of creative communities. Attend events, join groups, in person or virtual, and interact with peers. Engage sincerely—that's what binds people to you

I hate pitching myself.

That's normal, but you have to do it anyway. A good pitch doesn't boast; it's about connecting. Research who you're approaching and tailor your pitch to show how your work aligns with their goals. If you're a screenwriter pitching to a producer, highlight why your script fits their vision or fills a gap in their slate. If you're an artist, explain how your style complements the gallery's aesthetic. Keep it concise and specific.

Negotiation is part of the process. Learn to discuss rates, timelines, and deliverables with confidence. Practice saying your rates out loud: "My fee for this project is $1,500." The more you say it, the more natural it becomes. And always track your outreach (I use Google Sheets, for example). Organization is the difference between a one-time effort and a sustained strategy.

If I get an agent, do I still need to do this?

Absolutely. Agents close deals, but they don't create every opportunity for you. Keep hustling, keep building relationships, and keep finding your own doors to open. When you land an agent, collaborate with them. Keep them informed about your goals and any leads you're pursuing. The better they understand your vision, the more effectively they can support you.

Issa Rae didn't wait for Hollywood's approval. Before *Insecure*, she built her audience through *Awkward Black Girl*, a web series she produced and promoted herself. Reese Witherspoon saw the lack of female-driven stories in Hollywood and launched her own production company, Hello Sunshine, to take control of the narrative.

So I really have to take charge of my career?

Yes. Being your own agent isn't about doing everything alone; it's about taking ownership. When you advocate for yourself, you build confidence, credibility, and connections. And when opportunities come, you'll know you earned them. Because you championed yourself.

I get it. But what happens when I land an opportunity? How do I make sure I'm getting a fair deal?

55

NEGOTIATING FOR YOURSELF

I don't want to seem greedy.

That's a common fear. Many creatives hesitate to negotiate because they worry about coming across as difficult or demanding. Let's reframe. Negotiation is not about greed, and it is not about you. It is about clarity, respect, and making sure both parties get a fair deal. When done with professionalism, it strengthens relationships rather than straining them.

What if they say no?

They might. And that's okay. Negotiation is conversation. A back-and-forth where you align your value with what the other party needs. You will be creating an agreement that works for both sides.

But aren't negotiations supposed to be uncomfortable?

Only if you approach them like a battle. Instead, think of them as an exchange. The other person needs something you offer. You need to be compensated fairly. The best negotiations aren't about getting the most money possible; they're about making sure both sides walk away feeling good about the deal.

I still don't know how to start.

Negotiation begins with knowing your worth. Before you walk into any negotiation, ask yourself: What makes my work valuable? Why should they pay for it? Practice saying it out loud.. If you can't confidently explain your value, you'll struggle to defend it when negotiating. Like this:

Client: "We'd love to work with you, but our budget is tight. Can you do it for less?"

You: "I understand budget constraints, and I always aim to be flexible. My standard rate for this work is $2,500. If we need to adjust, we can discuss reducing the scope to match your budget."

Notice what you didn't do: You didn't apologize, you didn't immediately lower your price, and you didn't let the client dictate your worth. You stayed firm but open to solutions.

What if they ask me to name my price first?

That's actually an advantage. The first number named in a negotiation—this is called "anchoring"—shapes the entire conversation. If you say $3,000, they'll negotiate around that number. If they say $1,500 first, the discussion starts lower. Like this:

Client: "What's your rate for this project?"

You: "For a project of this scope, my fee is $3,000." (Pause. Don't rush to explain or justify.)

Client: "That's more than we were expecting."

You: "I understand. What's your budget range? Let's see if we can align expectations with what's possible."

You've set the bar while showing flexibility. Now, instead of just haggling, you're working toward a fair compromise.

What if I have no idea what to charge?

Do your homework. Look at industry standards. Ask peers. Whatever you think is fair, add 20 percent. Most creatives underprice themselves, and clients often expect to negotiate down.

What if they say they can't afford me?

That's their problem, not yours. If a client genuinely values your work, they'll find a way to meet your rate—or at least offer fair compensation. If they don't, that's a red flag. Like this:

Client: "We love your work, but we can only pay $500."

You: "Thanks for thinking of me! My rate for this type of project is $2,000. If that's beyond your budget, I'd be happy to recommend someone else who might be a better fit."

Notice how this keeps the door open while reinforcing your value. Clients often find extra budget when they see you won't accept less.

I'm scared of walking away from work.

Walking away is part of the process. If a deal isn't fair, it's better to decline than to resent the work later. Saying "no" doesn't mean you'll never get another opportunity. It means you're protecting your future time and energy. Like this:

Client: "This is a great opportunity for exposure."

You: "I appreciate that, but I've found that paid opportunities allow me to do my best work. Let me know if your budget changes."

Exposure doesn't pay the rent. Stand firm.

I get it. But what happens if a project falls through?

56

KILL FEES

I put so much time into this, and now they're just canceling? What about all my work?

Ah, yes. The infamous creative heartbreak. You commit, you dive in, you sweat over the details. Then, out of nowhere, the project vanishes. Maybe the client changes their mind. Maybe budgets shift. Maybe they just disappear into the void, never to be heard from again. Now you're standing there, unpaid, holding a half-finished project that no one will ever see.

Which is why we need to talk about kill fees.

I hate the name. It sounds so… final.

It's not as grim as it sounds. A kill fee is a safety net, not a death sentence! It's a clause in your contract that says if this project gets canceled, you still get paid for the work you've done. Because your time, your energy, and your creative labor don't become worthless just because someone changed their plans. A kill fee isn't a favor. It's a professional standard.

Creatives do the work before getting fully paid. Unlike buying a product off a shelf, where money changes hands instantly, the creative process requires trust. Trust that, at the end of all this effort, the client will follow through. But what happens when they don't? A kill fee ensures that no matter what, you don't walk away empty-handed. It also discourages clients from treating your time as disposable. A client who knows they'll have to pay something is a client who thinks twice before pulling the plug.

So… how do I make sure I actually get a kill fee?

You put it in writing.

Picture this: You're negotiating a new project. You talk about timelines, deliverables, the exciting things you'll create. Somewhere in that conversation, you casually mention: "Oh, by the way, if the project gets canceled, my standard kill fee is 30 percent."

No drama. No tension. Just business.

This is how professionals operate. Your mechanic charges a diagnostic fee even if you don't get your car fixed. A caterer still gets paid if you cancel the wedding last minute. You, my friend, are no different.

But what if they push back? What if they say, "We don't do that"?

Then you educate them: "Kill fees are common in creative work because we invest time up front. This ensures fairness for both of us while still giving you flexibility."

Most reasonable clients won't argue. The ones who do? Red flag. If someone resists a kill fee, they're basically saying, "I want the right to waste your time without consequence." And that's not someone you want to work with.

How much should a kill fee be?

It depends. Some people set it as a percentage of the total fee—anywhere from 25 to 50 percent, depending on how much work is already done. Others base it on actual work completed: For example, if you're halfway finished, you get half your fee. A tiered approach works well. If the project is canceled early, say in the first 25 percent of the timeline, a 30 percent kill fee applies. If it's halfway through, 50 percent is fair.

If it's nearly done, the full fee should be due. That way, compensation reflects effort.

Okay, but let's say the worst happens. They cancel, and they refuse to pay. Then what?

That's where contracts come in.

Let's talk about Malik, a designer I know. He landed a big branding and packaging project for a new beverage company. The client was enthusiastic, sending mood boards, talking big about their launch. Malik got to work. Weeks in, he sent over drafts. The client loved them.

And then, radio silence.

Eventually, he got an email: "We've decided to go in another direction. Thanks for your time!"

No mention of payment. No acknowledgment of the work he had already done.

But Malik had a contract. With a 50 percent kill fee. He responded professionally: "Per our agreement, the kill fee of 50 percent applies in case of project cancellation. Please find the final invoice attached."

They paid. No argument. No drama. Because it was in writing.

Okay, I see the point. But won't this scare off clients?

Not the good ones. Professional clients expect contracts, and a contract without a kill fee is an incomplete contract.

The way to make it standard is simple. Start putting kill fees in every contract, no exceptions. Introduce them casually, making them sound as standard as payment terms. Stick to them. If a client cancels, enforce the clause. If they push back, remind them that they agreed to it. Be firm, professional, and smile when you're reminding them.

And what if they say they don't work with kill fees at all?

Then ask yourself: Am I willing to take the risk of working without protection? Because it is a risk. A gamble on someone else's reliability.

When it comes to your time and effort, why gamble at all?

A kill fee isn't just about money. It's about respect. Respect for your work, your time, and your effort.

A kill fee says: If you cancel, that's fine. But my time still counts.

That's a boundary worth setting. In writing.

But we trust each other. Do I really need a contract?

57

GET IT IN WRITING

You need a contract. Every single time.

It's tempting to believe that a handshake, a friendly email, or a verbal promise will be enough. After all, you're working with people who respect you, right? They're excited about your work, they seem honest, and besides, you'd rather focus on the creative part than get bogged down in legalese.

Contracts feel stiff. They feel like something corporate lawyers in suits haggle over in boardrooms, not something that belongs in the world of artists, writers, and musicians. Reality check: Getting it in writing is one of the most powerful things you can do for yourself and your work. Something in writing will provide clarity and protection and ensure that everyone understands the terms of the creative partnership before problems arise.

Because problems will arise.

Think of a contract like a road map. It lays out where you're going, how you'll get there, and what happens if someone takes an unexpected detour. It keeps misunderstandings from turning into conflicts, and it saves you from the nightmare of chasing down payment, dealing with scope creep, or, in a worst-case scenario, watching your work get used in ways you never agreed to.

Without a contract, you might hear, "I thought you were delivering five designs, not just two!" With a contract, it's clear from the start: "Per our agreement, the project includes two finalized designs." No confusion, no last-minute panic.

A contract also protects your work. You spend weeks, maybe months, creating something meaningful. Then, suddenly, the client ghosts you. No payment, no explanation, just radio silence. Without a written agreement, you have no leverage. With one, you have legal proof that they owe you for the work you've already done.

Scope creep is another danger. A project starts small, then suddenly balloons into something ten times bigger. The client keeps asking for "just one more thing." If you don't have a contract defining what's included (and what isn't), you'll find yourself doing twice the work for the same pay. With a contract, it's simple: "Revisions beyond the agreed two rounds will incur an additional fee of $X per round." Now, if they want more, they'll need to pay more.

Every agreement should cover the essentials: the scope of work, payment terms, ownership and rights, a kill fee in case of cancellation, deadlines and delivery, and what happens if something goes wrong. Who owns the final work? Do you retain copyright, or are you transferring rights? When will the work be completed? What's expected from the client in terms of feedback? If a dispute arises, how will it be handled? These are not small details. They are the framework that keeps a project running smoothly.

I have learned this lesson the hard way. Early in my indie producing life, I agreed to help a rich guy evaluate movie projects he might invest in. I spent a ton of time doing research, comparisons, and sourcing projects he could consider. We had a handshake on how he'd pay me for my time. Then he ghosted me. After that, I started using contracts for every job, and I never had that problem again. The contract also smokes out the person who won't pay you in the end; if they balk at having a contract, they have told you all you need to know.

Lin-Manuel Miranda, before *Hamilton* became a phenomenon, made sure every aspect of ownership and royalties was outlined in detailed contracts. These agreements ensured he retained control over his work and its future earnings. Without them, he might have lost creative and financial ownership of one of the most successful musicals of all time.

A contract doesn't have to be twenty pages long, but it should cover the key points. And it needs to be signed. A contract isn't enforceable unless both parties sign it.

A contract ensures fairness, respect, and clarity for everyone involved. It protects your creative efforts, your time, and your career. The best collaborations are built on transparency and trust, and a written agreement ensures that trust is well-placed.

Do I need a lawyer for my contracts?

58

YES, YOU NEED A LAWYER

But I'm just starting out. I don't have the money for a lawyer.

I hear you. Hiring a lawyer sounds like something only big-time creatives do, the ones signing major record deals or negotiating Hollywood contracts. I'm not an attorney, but I will give you this one piece of legal advice: The sooner you get legal counsel, the fewer expensive mistakes you'll have to fix later. Legal mistakes can be brutal. You can lose rights to your own work and even your own name, you can get stuck in a bad contract, you can spend years fighting for payment you were promised.

If you're creating work that has value, you need legal protection. The good news is that there are ways to get it without breaking the bank.

Do I really need legal advice already? It's not like I have a huge deal on the table.

If you're working with clients, signing agreements, or collaborating on projects, legal issues will come up. The question is whether you'll be prepared or blindsided. Clients have lawyers reviewing their contracts before they send them your way. If you sign without understanding the fine print, you're agreeing to terms designed to protect them, not you. That's how business works. Their job is to look out for themselves; your job is to look out for you. Looking out for yourself starts with knowing what you're signing.

Can't I can just read it over myself?

You can try, but legal language is deliberately dense. You might think a contract says one thing when, in reality, a single clause buried on page three means something else entirely. Early-career screenwriters come to me with this all the time. A producer offered to option their script. The contract seemed straightforward, so they signed without legal help. Months later, they realized they had given away unlimited rights for years into the future. Even if the producer sits on the project these screenwriters can't do anything; and if the movie is ever made, they will have left substantial rights and money on the table. The cost either to try to fix or in lost income? Tens of thousands. The cost of avoiding it up front? A couple grand.

If you're collaborating, signing deals, or licensing your work, legal protection ensures you get paid fairly and no one takes advantage of your creativity. Copyright, licensing, royalties, and contracts aren't just technicalities. They determine whether you control your own work or give it away without realizing it.

Legal problems are exhausting. The emotional toll alone—emailing back and forth, arguing over money, trying to decipher legal jargon—can take weeks of your life. A lawyer handles it so you don't have to. That means more time for your creative work and fewer sleepless nights.

But lawyers are expensive. What if I just can't afford one?

Not all legal help comes with high price tags. Some attorneys offer flat fees instead of hourly billing, so you know up front what you're paying for. Others will negotiate their rates based on your budget or offer payment plans. You should always ask for an estimate of what the legal fees will be, and it's okay to shop around. Plus, AI-empowered law is driving down the price of legal expenses every day.

Hiring a lawyer doesn't need to be considered an expense. It is a source of greater revenue and protection, and a way to avoid big expenses later. Getting legal advice up front is like paying for insurance. You hope you won't need it, but you'll be grateful you have it when the time comes that you do need it.

I don't even know where to start. What kind of legal help do I actually need?

At a minimum, you need help reviewing contracts before you sign anything significant. If you're licensing your work, entering a publishing deal, or collaborating on a project, a lawyer ensures you retain ownership, get paid fairly, and aren't agreeing to something that could hurt you later. Over time, having a lawyer who understands your work will make it easier (and cheaper) to get help when you need it.

I'm sure you've listened to "Taylor's Version" of her early albums. That's because she signed a contract saying she didn't own or have any control over the masters of her recording sessions, and then, over her profound objections, her masters were sold. She recorded her early albums to make her own version, which she controls. Legal foresight matters. Richard Prince, a visual artist, has been sued multiple times over the use of copyrighted images in his work. Understanding intellectual property law early could have saved him from legal headaches. Ava DuVernay has used legal contracts to maintain creative control over her projects. Strong legal support has allowed her to dictate the terms of her career rather than having them dictated to her.

I guess I just don't feel like I'm "big enough" to need a lawyer yet.

That's exactly why now is the time. When you start setting good legal habits early, you prevent problems before they happen. Book a consultation—many lawyers offer a free or low-cost first meeting, and even a single conversation can give you clarity. Be up front about costs—ask for clear pricing and explore options like flat fees or payment plans. You don't need a lawyer for every email you send, but for contracts, licensing deals, or anything involving ownership rights, professional guidance is a must.

A lawyer isn't a luxury—it's a necessity if you're serious about your creative career. Whether you're licensing a song, signing a publishing deal, or collaborating on a project, legal protection ensures you retain control over your work and get what you're owed.

And remember this: If a client has a lawyer, that means you need one, too.

Okay, I get it. Contracts, ownership, getting legal help. This is serious. But what about the times when people ask me to work for free? Sometimes I feel like I have to say "yes" just to get my foot in the door.

59

WHEN TO WORK FOR FREE

"Never work for free." "Always work for free to get your name out there." I've heard both. Which one is right?

Neither. And both. It's not that simple.

Some people say never take unpaid work because they've been burned by clients promising exposure that never materializes, endless "opportunities" that somehow never lead to anything real. Others swear by free projects because they've led to career breakthroughs.

Free work isn't inherently good or bad. It depends on when, why, and how you do it. If you know what you're getting, and that it actually serves you, then working for free can be a smart move. If not? Walk away.

I thought working for free meant being taken advantage of.

Not necessarily. Sometimes, free work is an investment of your time, talent, and energy. But like any investment, it has to offer something in return. Otherwise, you're just giving away your work for nothing. A good return could be an opportunity to connect with people or spaces you couldn't reach otherwise. It might be skill-building, working in a new medium, testing ideas, refining your craft. It might be alignment, creating something that matters to you, even if money isn't involved. It might be visibility, but only when it's real and not just an empty promise of "exposure."

Give me a real example.

A photographer volunteers for a nonprofit's gala, and their images end up in major magazines. A playwright self-produces a no-budget solo show, and it turns into an Emmy-winning TV series. An artist paints a free mural in a public space, and suddenly they're getting commissioned for large-scale work. These aren't hypotheticals. They're real stories from creatives who made unpaid work work for them.

So how do I know if it's worth it?

Ask yourself: Does this serve your long-term goals? Will it help you get where you want to go? Does it put you in front of the right people? Not just any audience, the right audience? Does it let you practice your craft in a meaningful way? Some skills you only get by doing. Does it bring you joy, stretch your abilities, or align with your values? Passion projects count. If the answer is "yes" to any of these, it might be worth your time. But only if you choose it on your terms.

What about "exposure"? Doesn't that count?

Yes, but only if it's real. Too often, offering "exposure" is a smoke-screen for getting free labor without giving you anything of real value. So if someone tells you a project will give you exposure, ask: How big is the audience? Are we talking ten people or ten thousand? Will my work be properly credited? Will my name, website, or social media be featured? Are people in my industry actually going to see this? Because "general audience" isn't always helpful. If they can't give specifics, it's not real exposure. It's just an excuse not to pay you.

So when should I turn it down?

When the answer to "What am I getting out of this?" is "nothing." If the only person benefiting is the other party. If it drains your time, energy, creative bandwidth without giving back, free work will deplete your creative reserves. Free work shouldn't replace income.

What if it's for a friend?

That depends. Are they the kind of friend who truly values what you do? Or do they just assume your skills are a favor they're entitled to? Gratitude and respect matter. If someone expects free work without acknowledgment, that's a red flag.

How do I decide?

Before saying "yes" to unpaid work, ask yourself: What's the reward? Is it real value beyond money—for example, experience, exposure, connections, fulfillment? Who benefits? Am I gaining something, or is this just free labor for someone else? Can I afford it—financially, emotionally, creatively? Does this cost me more than it gives?

Before becoming the first artist to win a Grammy for a streaming-only album, Chance the Rapper gave away his first albums for free, to introduce his work to his audience and learn how they responded. Visual artist Mark Bradford freely provides his time and mentors emerging artists, and he donated a large space to bring cultural programming to his neighborhood of Leimert Park. Phoebe Waller-Bridge started *Fleabag* as a one-woman fringe show, with no budget and no guarantees, but it led to a TV deal, an Emmy, and a defining career moment.

Working for free isn't about devaluing yourself. It's about knowing when the value lies beyond money. Sometimes it's about experience. Sometimes it's about opportunity. Sometimes it's about creative fulfillment. But the key? Make sure it's your choice.

I've talked to some friends about creating something together. How could that work?

60

COLLABORATIONS AND PARTNERSHIPS

There's something intoxicating about a great creative partnership. Ideas bounce, momentum builds, and suddenly, you're creating something that neither of you could have done alone. The best collaborations elevate your work, expand your reach, and stretch your thinking.

And the worst? They crash, burn, and leave behind resentment, lost work, and sometimes even legal headaches.

So how do I make sure I get the first kind and not the second?

By treating your collaboration like what it is: a business relationship. That doesn't mean you kill the creative spark with paperwork and rules. It means you set the right foundation so the work and the relationship survive success, stress, and everything in between.

We don't need a contract to collaborate—we're friends.

I hear this one all the time. And sure, when things are going well, you don't think you need anything in writing. But what happens when there's money on the table? When one person is putting in more effort than the other? When one of you wants to take the work in a different direction? A written agreement will make sure you both feel secure, respected, and aligned.

Imagine a photographer and a chef team up to create a cookbook. The book does well—really well. But who owns the images? Who owns the text? Can one person take their part and use it elsewhere? Without a contract, they might end up in a legal battle that could have been avoided with one up-front conversation.

Okay, but what should go in this agreement?

Ownership needs to be clear—who owns what and whether contributions are shared equally or separately. It should cover revenue sharing so that profits, royalties, or future earnings are distributed fairly. It should define decision-making authority, who has the final say, and what happens if there's a disagreement. It should outline credit, so there's no confusion about how each person will be acknowledged in marketing, promotions, and the final work. And it needs an exit plan. If one person leaves, what happens to the project? Can they use their part separately, or does everything remain jointly owned?

I don't want to bring up contracts. It'll ruin the creative vibe.

Actually, it does the opposite. When everything is clear up front, you don't have to worry about misunderstandings derailing the project later. The best way to handle this is to normalize these conversations from the start.

So we just put some basic terms in writing so we're both protected.

That's it. Simple. If your collaborator resists that? Red flag. And if conversations get tricky, bring in a neutral third party. A lawyer, a mentor, or even a template from a reputable source.

Do we need to start a business entity together?

Not usually. A formal LLC or corporation can be overkill for most collaborations. Start with a simple written agreement before diving into complex legal structures. If things grow, you can always evolve the partnership later.

Let's talk about Matt Damon and Ben Affleck, two guys who wrote *Good Will Hunting* together and made sure their roles were clear. They had equal credit, clear ownership, and knew how they wanted to handle success. Compare that to The Beatles, a legendary collaboration, but with vague agreements that led to disputes over ownership and rights for decades after the band split.

Collaboration works best when trust and clarity exist together. You will be protecting yourself, the work, the friendship, and the future of what you're building. Because the last thing you want is a brilliant, successful project… that ends in a fight over who owns it.

Okay, I am going to make sure I have the right collaborators. Then what?

61

BUILD AND SUPPORT YOUR TEAM

A good place to start is recognizing that you can't do everything alone. No one does. Not the greatest artists, filmmakers, musicians, or writers. The most successful creatives build teams that amplify their vision, because the best teams make your work better than you ever imagined.

But I don't have the budget to hire a full team.

You don't need a big team. You need the right people at the right time. Maybe it's one collaborator, maybe two. Maybe it's swapping skills with someone instead of paying them. Maybe it's hiring a freelancer for just a few hours a week. You start small and build intentionally. With the right people.

How do I even know who I need?

Start by looking at yourself. What are you great at? What do you love doing? Then ask: What drains you? What distracts you from the work only you can do? Be honest. If marketing feels like pulling teeth, bring in someone who loves it. If managing schedules makes you want to run for the hills, find an assistant. Your time and energy are too valuable to spend on things that someone else could do better and faster.

Okay, let's say I find the right people. How do I make sure we actually work well together?

That's where leadership comes in. Being a creative also means being a people-manager. A great team is nurtured. If people feel valued, they'll bring their best. If they feel like cogs in a machine, they'll check out or walk away.

So… how do I keep them invested?

You communicate. Clearly, consistently, and with respect. Tell them the Why behind your decisions. Ask for their input. Treat them like creative partners. And when they do great work, say it. A simple "thank you" matters. Public recognition matters even more.

And if they're not delivering?

Then you address it. Directly, but constructively. Don't let resentment build. If someone isn't meeting expectations, talk to them. Maybe they need more clarity. Maybe they need to be in a different role. Maybe they're just not the right fit. The best teams evolve, and sometimes that means letting go of what doesn't work.

This sounds like a lot of work.

It is. But think about what happens if you don't build a team. You do everything yourself. You burn out. You stall. Your work suffers. That's the real cost.

Fine, you convinced me. Who actually does this well?

I hope I do. When I'm producing a movie, there is no way I could do it all—I don't have the expertise and we need lots of people. I bring together the best director, writer, actors, cinematographer, designers, and crew I can find. Beyoncé surrounds herself with a powerhouse team:

producers, designers, and choreographers who elevate her performances into cultural moments. Guillermo del Toro gives his designers creative freedom, trusting them to push boundaries: That's how *The Shape of Water* ended up looking like nothing else.

What's the common thread? Supporting the talented people we find.

Okay, so where do I start?

Start small. Maybe it's one person. Maybe it's a collaborator who balances your strengths. Maybe it's a virtual assistant who takes one task off your plate. The goal isn't to build an empire overnight. It's to free yourself up to do what only you can do.

And if I mess up? If it doesn't work?

Then you learn. You adjust. You try again. That's what creative work is, after all. Experimenting, refining, evolving. Your team is no different.

What if I pick the wrong people?

62

WHEN PEOPLE DON'T DO WHAT THEY SAY THEY WILL DO

People miss deadlines. They say "yes," then life happens. Or they mean well, but they overpromise. Or they just don't prioritize.

So what do you do? You don't let it slide. If you let one missed deadline go, you're inviting more.

But I don't want to be pushy.

Again, reframe: This is being professional. Your work depends on other people doing what they said they would. If they don't, your project suffers. So the first step is setting expectations early. Be specific. Instead of "Can you get me the draft by Friday?" say: "The draft is due Friday by 5:00 p.m. If there are any issues, let me know by Wednesday so we can adjust."

Even better: Share the big picture on when your project needs to hit its milestones, then let your collaborators build the schedule with you. Ask them when they can have each item ready. Chances are, they will set a deadline even sooner than you would have asked, and they will stick to it because they set it themselves. And then, if they miss it, there's no confusion. You had an agreement.

Okay, but what if they still don't deliver?

Then you address it immediately. No waiting, no hoping they'll magically remember. A simple, direct check-in works, like "I didn't receive the file yesterday as planned. Where are we with this?"

Most people, when called out, will either fix the problem or explain what went wrong. If they make excuses, hold them accountable.

I could say: "We agreed on this deadline. How do we get back on track?"

Good. That way you're not attacking a person. You're keeping the project moving.

What if this keeps happening?

Then it's a pattern. Document everything. After every missed deadline, follow up in writing: "As discussed, you'll deliver the final draft by Monday at noon. Let's check in that morning to ensure we're on schedule."

If it happens again, you now have proof. At that point, you escalate: "This is the second time we've missed a deadline. What's going on?"

Some people just aren't reliable. When that's the case, you have to make a decision.

Let them go?

Yes. If someone consistently doesn't follow through, they're hurting the project. Letting them go isn't about punishment—it's about protecting the work.

On the movies and theater I have produced, there have been times I had to relieve someone of their position. Once it was a man who was old enough to be my dad, who had actually been my teacher in college, because he was showing up drunk. Once it was a prop-master who never had the actors' props on time, and then showed up on set with a real gun—not a prop gun that had been modified so it could not fire live rounds. (That was instant dismissal. No live guns on the set—ever.) Sometimes I have had to replace writers and actors. When this happens,

I comport myself with love and compassion, and I stay true to my purpose, which is to be on the side of the project, not a person or personality. This is what's necessary to make your creative work strong. Because it's not personal. It's business.

But what if they have a good reason?

Life happens. If someone is struggling, lead with empathy: "I've noticed deadlines have been slipping. Is there something going on? How can we adjust?"

Sometimes they need flexibility. Sometimes they need to step back. Either way, you're handling it instead of ignoring it.

And if I don't handle it?

Then you'll spend more time fixing problems than creating great work. And that's not the job.

Okay, I get it. But what if someone just walks away? No notice, no explanation—just disappears? I put all this effort into building a great team, and then they just… leave?

63

WHEN PEOPLE QUIT ON YOU

It happens. No matter how well you choose your people, no matter how carefully you set things up, someone will eventually quit. Sometimes it's graceful. Sometimes it's messy. But it will happen, and when it does, you'll have a choice. Take it personally, or take it in stride.

It feels personal, though.

Of course it does. You trusted them. You relied on them. You assumed they were in it for the long haul, and now they're walking away. It can feel like a rejection of you, your work, or your vision. But in almost every case, it's not about you. People leave projects for their own reasons—burnout, shifting priorities, better opportunities, or simply realizing they weren't as invested as they thought.

Your job isn't to dwell on why they're leaving. Your job is to make sure their departure doesn't derail everything.

So what do I do first?

You breathe. Reacting emotionally won't help. Before you say anything, take a step back. Let yourself feel whatever frustration or disappointment comes up, but don't act on it. The last thing you need is a conversation fueled by hurt feelings.

Once you've centered yourself, have the conversation. If they've already decided to leave, don't waste energy trying to change their mind. Instead, focus on a smooth transition. Say something like "I appreciate what you've contributed, and I understand you need to move on. Let's make a plan to wrap up your part so we can move forward without disruption."

This does two things. First, it acknowledges their decision with professionalism, instead of turning it into a fight. Second, it makes it clear that quitting doesn't mean they can just walk away without tying up loose ends.

What if they're not actually quitting, just... disappearing?

Then you call it what it is. If someone is disengaging, missing deadlines, or doing the bare minimum, have the conversation before it gets worse.

Say to them, "I've noticed you're less engaged lately. Is everything okay?"

Sometimes, they'll admit they're struggling. Maybe they're overwhelmed or dealing with personal issues. If that's the case, you can adjust—redistribute their workload, extend a deadline, or help them step back without harming the project.

Other times, they'll dodge, make excuses, or insist everything is fine, while still not delivering. That's when you set a clear boundary: "I need to know if you're fully committed. If not, we need to figure out an exit plan now rather than let things drag on."

This forces a decision. If they want to stay, they have to step up. If they don't, you move forward without them.

What if their quitting really does mess everything up?

It might, temporarily. But every project has its setbacks. The key is to triage the damage. If it is a digital project, make sure you have the usernames, passwords, and two-factor-authentication numbers of everyone on your team, so you can have access if someone departs. Then ask yourself or your team: What's unfinished? What needs immediate attention? Can someone else take over, even in the short term?

And document everything. Before they leave, get their files, their notes, anything they've worked on. The last thing you want is to be hunting down missing pieces after they're gone.

What if I'm just… done? I don't want to keep rebuilding a team every time someone leaves.

That's valid. Losing people is exhausting. But the work still needs to get done. This is why every great leader, from George Lucas to Shonda Rhimes, builds systems that make their projects bigger than any one person. They know people will come and go, so they create processes that keep things moving. They also know that voluntary attrition can spread like a cold—one person leaving can incite another's departure. This is when leadership makes a profound difference; by holding the remaining team together, you build trust and strengthen continuity.

If it happens, learn from each loss. Check in with the rest of your team, articulate your vision with passion and charisma to reignite enthusiasm, improve your hiring instincts, and put better structures in place so the next time someone quits, it won't feel like the whole thing is falling apart.

And if it happens again?

Then you keep going. Maybe with some tech to come to the rescue.

I keep hearing that AI is going to take over everything. Is that true?

64

AI AND TECHNOLOGY FOR CREATIVE LIFE

Every creative, in every era, faces a new technology that disrupts the landscape when it arrives, and suddenly, everyone panics. It happened when photography challenged painting, when synthesizers shook up music, when digital tools transformed design. Now, it's AI. And just like every innovation before it, AI will change, not replace creativity. The question isn't whether AI will reshape creative work. It already has. The real question is how you'll use it to your advantage.

AI can generate, analyze, optimize. It cannot dream. While AI can create outputs that appear like dreaming, joy, heartbreak, curiosity, it cannot feel those emotions.

I suspect that our relationship to AI's work product will mirror the development of visual effects in film. In 1987, when I saw Brian DePalma's film *The Untouchables*, Frank Nitti's fall off the roof looked great. Today I see it as a cheesy visual effect.

When Photoshop became mainstream, did great designers disappear? No, but generic, amateur design became easier to spot. AI will do the same for creative work.

Likewise, I predict that as AI becomes more commonplace, we will become more attuned to its attributes, be more able to identify what is AI and what is not, and seek the human touch more deeply.

AI can assemble ideas, but it doesn't have lived experience. That's your edge. AI might be able to remix melodies, draft scripts, or generate concept art, but only you can infuse meaning into it. Creative work is 10 percent technology and technique, 90 percent people. AI will make the technique and technology faster, better, easier. But it will not be the variegated human experience, shaped by history, culture, and emotions.

So where does AI actually help?

It helps by making your process faster, smoother, and more efficient. Think about the hours spent on admin work, revisions, scheduling, and logistics. None of that is why you became a creative. AI can transcribe notes, suggest color palettes, organize your calendar, and automate invoicing. The less time you spend on busywork, the more time you have to create. Filmmakers use AI to generate instant concept art, set up shots, and do visual effects. Musicians use it to assist with mixing. Writers use it to brainstorm, refine, and iterate. The final creative determinations belong to humans.

But doesn't that mean the market will be flooded with AI-generated content?

Yes. That's more of a threat to democracy and our social fabric than to creativity. In fact, I hope so much fake and disinformation AI floods the zone that we will feel overwhelmed by it. Then, by our nature, we will start to seek verifiable sources of truth. But we will need to pass through this uncomfortable AI-flood first.

So how do I use AI without losing my creative integrity?

First, master the tools instead of fearing them. Run toward AI and embrace it. Understand how AI works, so you're the one in control. Let AI handle the mechanical parts of your workflow, but keep your creative choices human. Use AI to explore possibilities, but make the final call based on your instinct and experience. AI might be able to generate a thousand logo variations in minutes, but only you can decide which one truly communicates the story you want to tell.

Second, lean in to emotional depth. AI can analyze trends, but it can't create something personal, vulnerable, or risky. That's your lane. If AI can churn out polished, predictable content, then unpredictable, deeply personal work will be what audiences will value most.

Third, shift toward experiences. AI struggles with real-world interaction, live performance, and collaborative energy. Focus on the things that require a human presence—storytelling that surprises, art that invites participation, music that makes people feel something beyond algorithmic perfection.

What about using AI for business?

AI is the perfect business partner. It can automate client communications, track finances, and optimize marketing. Social media tools powered by AI can analyze trends, predict engagement, and schedule content for maximum impact. AI can help creatives scale their work, allowing a designer to mock up ideas faster, a filmmaker to refine storyboards instantly, or a musician to experiment with mixing before heading into the studio.

Okay, but what happens when AI gets even better? What if it can do everything?

Then the same rule applies: Creativity isn't just about execution. It's about the choices you make, the risks you take, and the meaning behind your work. As AI gets better, you need to get better, too, by refining your instincts, your perspective, and your ability to create work that feels undeniably human.

Beeple used digital tools, and later AI, to create groundbreaking digital art, but his vision is what made his work valuable. Jessica Walsh integrates AI-generated elements into her designs, but it's her taste and craftsmanship that define the final product. Grimes collaborates with AI to compose music, but the storytelling and emotion? That's all her. The future of creativity isn't about competing with AI. It's about using AI's strengths to amplify your own.

Lean in to what makes you human. Let technology be your partner. The creatives who thrive will be the ones who make AI work for them.

So how much should I spend on my technology partner?

65

EVERY DOLLAR IS A DECISION

Every creative spends money, but the way you spend it determines whether your career grows or stalls. The difference between an investment and an expense is simple but powerful: Investments pay you back. They generate income, sharpen your skills, or open doors. Expenses, while sometimes unavoidable, drain your resources without creating long-term value.

But how do I know which is which?

This is where most creatives get stuck. It's easy to convince yourself that anything connected to your craft is an investment. But the test is whether it creates a return.

What about things like rent or software?

Some expenses are necessary just to keep going. You need a place to live, tools to do your work, and maybe even a coffee to get through the afternoon. But even here, you can tell which ones support your future. A designer subscribing to a software package is making an investment: It's a tool that pays for itself over years of use. A writer buying an expensive leather notebook for ideas? That's just a luxury.

So how do I make smart spending choices?

Before you buy anything, ask: Will this pay off financially or professionally? Will it move me closer to my next milestone? Can I afford it without compromising something more important? If you're not sure, wait. The best investments hold their value over time.

What if I want something, even if it's not an investment?

Then be honest with yourself. It's fine to buy something just because it makes you happy. Just don't confuse that with something that will advance your work. Splurging on a workspace you don't really need? Expense. Paying for a class that improves your craft? Investment. A flashy, overpriced microphone that doesn't make your work better? Expense. A high-quality microphone that helps you book paid gigs? Investment.

Who really does this well?

Tyler Perry reinvested profits from his stage plays into building his own studio, which gave him complete creative control. Issa Rae self-funded *Awkward Black Girl*, proving that a well-placed investment in your own work can lead to breakthrough opportunities, like her HBO deal. Quincy Jones built wealth by owning his music catalogs, turning early earnings into royalties that lasted for decades. They didn't just spend; they invested in what truly mattered.

What if I don't have much to invest?

Start small. Test before committing. Use what you already have. Shoot video on your phone before buying a $3,000 camera. Track where your money goes and, every few months, look at what's working. Which purchases actually helped your career? Which ones weren't worth it? Over time, this awareness makes you a sharper, smarter investor in your own future.

Every financial decision either moves you toward creative independence or keeps you stuck. The sooner you start, the sooner you'll have a foundation strong enough to support your creative life on your terms.

Great. What's the best way for me to get paid?

66

INVOICING

You've done the work. You've delivered. Now comes the part that actually makes it all worth it: getting paid. It should be simple: Send an invoice, get the money. But if you've been in this business for any length of time, you know it rarely goes that smoothly.

Do I really need to be that formal? Can't I just send a quick email saying, "Hey, can you Venmo me?"

You can do that. And if it's a casual gig with a friend, maybe that's fine. But if you want to get paid consistently and on time, you need a system. A proper invoice signals that payment isn't optional, and it gives you a record to stand on if things go sideways.

A good invoice makes it as easy as possible for your client to pay you. Your name and contact details go at the top, followed by the client's. In larger companies, invoices get passed around, so it's critical that yours lands in front of the right person. Every invoice should also have a unique invoice number, making it easier to track payments. Use a system so it isn't random: sequential numbers, dates, whatever works for you.

Always include the date the invoice is sent and the due date. Standard terms like "Net 15" or "Net 30" mean payment is due in fifteen or thirty days, but if you need faster payment, say "Due Upon Receipt." And be specific in the description. Instead of "graphic design work," write "brand identity package, including three initial concepts, final design, and two rounds of revisions." The more details, the less room for misunderstandings.

Clearly state the total amount due and list your payment methods. Make it simple: If you accept bank transfers, include the details. If you use PayPal, Venmo, or Stripe, add the link. Some clients still prefer paper checks, and if that's the case, tell them where to send it. And don't forget a short note at the end. A simple "Thank you for your business" adds a professional touch, while a clear late-payment policy sets expectations up front.

Okay, but how do I actually make sure I get paid?

Send your invoice immediately. The longer you wait, the easier it is for clients to push it to the back of the line. Invoicing apps and software will streamline this for you. These platforms create professional invoices, send automatic reminders, and track payments so you don't have to.

Do you do this?

I've learned the hard way that vague invoices lead to delays. Now, I invoice immediately, with clear descriptions and late-payment terms built in. I require a deposit before I start work. This smokes out the folk who will be jerks when it comes to collecting.

What should I do right now?

If you're not already using professional invoices, you can start today. Even if you only work with a few clients, having a system in place makes it easier to grow. Go through your past payment requests. Does anyone still owe you? Send a follow-up now. Don't hesitate. This is your money, and you earned it.

And if you're tired of chasing payments, consider requiring a deposit before you begin work. Many creatives ask for 50 percent up front, which ensures that at least part of your time is covered, no matter what happens.

Invoices will get you paid and place value on your time, setting the standard for how clients treat you. When you take it seriously, they will, too. Because the sooner they pay, the sooner you can get back to what actually matters: creating.

What if they don't pay?

67

WHAT TO DO WHEN YOU'RE NOT PAID ON TIME

You sent the invoice. The due date passed. No payment. No update. Just silence.

Maybe they just forgot? Maybe their accounting team is slow? Maybe they're hoping I won't notice?

It doesn't really matter why—it matters what you do next. And no, the answer isn't to sit around and hope.

Most late payments aren't malicious. Invoices get lost, internal systems are slow, or payments require multiple approvals. But some companies deliberately delay payments to hold on to cash longer, hoping freelancers won't push back. And in the worst cases, a client never intended to pay you at all. The key is not to panic and not to take it personally. This is business, and you have every right to follow up.

Start with a friendly reminder. Keep it professional and polite. Something like:

Hi [Client's Name], I hope you're doing well! Just following up on Invoice [#], which was due on [date]. Let me know if you need any details to process it. Looking forward to receiving payment soon. Best, [Your Name]

Most of the time, this gets things moving. People see the reminder, realize they forgot, and send the payment. But if nothing happens? Time to step it up.

A week later, follow up with a firmer message. No apologies, no hedging—just direct professionalism:

Hi [Client's Name], I wanted to check in again on Invoice [#], which was due on [date] and is now [X] days overdue. As per our agreement, late payments may be subject to [late fee if applicable]. Please confirm when I can expect payment. Thanks, [Your Name]

This makes it clear you're paying attention, and that delay isn't an option. If they still don't respond, it's time to escalate.

Emails are easy to ignore, but a phone call is harder to brush off. Call and ask directly when payment will be made. If that doesn't work, send a formal demand letter outlining the overdue amount, any late fees, and potential next steps. If the client claims financial hardship, you can offer a structured payment plan, but only if you trust them to follow through.

If none of that works, it's time for the final move: enforcement. Some creatives use collections agencies for large unpaid amounts, though they'll take a percentage of what's recovered. If the amount is significant, filing in small claims court may be worth it. And in extreme cases, going public—sharing warnings on social media or industry forums—can apply pressure, though it should always be a last resort due to potential legal implications.

Of course, the best way to deal with late payments is to prevent them in the first place. Require up-front deposits so you're never working entirely unpaid. Use contracts that spell out payment terms, due dates, and late fees clearly. Most importantly, vet your clients. If a company has a reputation for slow payments, think twice before taking the job.

Clients who don't pay hope you'll give up. Don't.

Chasing payments isn't fun, but enforcing your agreements and setting clear expectations makes it happen less often. The stronger your policies, the more professional you appear, and the less likely clients will think they can get away with delaying your paycheck. Your work is valuable. Your time is valuable. You deserve to be paid, on time, every time.

I feel like I should incorporate. It seems like a smart move. More official.

68

WHEN TO INCORPORATE

You've heard that incorporating is a rite of passage, the moment when you officially become a "real" creative professional. That's the myth, isn't it? But incorporating too soon is like putting a frame on an unfinished painting. It might look polished from the outside, but if the work isn't ready, what's the point?

A lot of people think a legal business structure will magically solve their problems. Clients will take you more seriously. You'll get paid more. Taxes will somehow work in your favor. But incorporation is just a tool. If you don't need it, it just adds extra work: filing fees, separate tax returns, and ongoing paperwork. If you're a solo creative working on small-scale projects, you're probably fine operating as a sole proprietor. A clear contract and smart financial habits will do more for you right now than an LLC or S-Corp ever could.

So when does it actually make sense to incorporate?

There are a few clear signs. If you're working with corporate partners, incorporation can define your ownership of your work, and it may even be a requirement for the company to work with you. Certain companies only work with incorporated vendors, and if that's blocking you from landing bigger gigs, it might be time.

Another sign is when your personal assets are at risk. If your work involves large investments—producing a film, launching a product, hiring a team—incorporation protects your personal finances. If the project fails, your savings and home stay separate from any debts or liabilities.

If your income is consistently growing, incorporation can also provide tax benefits. If you're making six figures from freelance work or licensing deals, a loan-out corporation could help you reduce taxable income and qualify for business deductions.

I've heard a little about loan-out corporations for creatives. What are they?

They are a type of corporation designed for individuals—writers, filmmakers, musicians—to manage their income under a business entity. Instead of you personally signing contracts, your corporation does. Payments go to the corporation, which then pays you a salary or distributions. It's useful for tax planning, business deductions, and credibility when dealing with studios or agencies. But again, it's only worth it when your income is steady and substantial.

When I started being an independent producer and business consultant, I set up my corporation. It's a loan-out corporation, optimizing taxes, and it helped me secure work with major studios. I didn't rush into incorporation. I waited until it was necessary, and that's what made it a strategic move, not just a symbolic one.

So how do I know if I'm ready?

Ask yourself: Am I working with partners who need defined financial roles? Is my income high enough that tax benefits would make a difference? Are my personal assets at risk? Am I losing work because I'm not incorporated?

If the answer is no, please wait. I have made the mistake of starting a new corporation too soon, only to discover the project didn't go, then I had to unwind the damn thing. Which cost more money. If the answer is yes, talk to a lawyer and accountant to make sure you're setting up the right structure.

So basically… don't do it just to feel legit.

Exactly. You're already legit. Incorporate only when you need to.

I have a big, ambitious project, but I'm not a nonprofit. Does that mean I can't apply for grants or accept tax-deductible donations?

69

WHAT ABOUT NONPROFITS?

As long as your project is truly for the public good, that's where a fiscal sponsor comes in. A fiscal sponsor is a nonprofit organization that lends its nonprofit status to your project. Think of it as a partnership: You handle the creative work, and the sponsor handles the administrative details, processing tax-deductible donations, managing compliance, and giving your project the kind of credibility that funders love.

So I get all the benefits of being a nonprofit without starting one?

Yes, but there will be some strings attached. Your project needs to align with the sponsor's mission, and there's usually an administrative fee, typically 5 to 15 percent of the funds you raise. That might sound like a lot, but in exchange, you gain access to grants, donors, and resources you wouldn't have on your own. More importantly, you get to focus on making your project happen without drowning in paperwork and legal complexities.

How does it actually work?

Let's say you're making a documentary about climate change, and an environmental nonprofit agrees to be your fiscal sponsor. When donors contribute, the money goes to the nonprofit, not you. They earmark those funds for your project, and you can access them as needed within the agreed terms. Your project remains creatively independent while you operate under their legal and tax umbrella.

That sounds great, but what's the catch?

There's no catch, just responsibilities. You have to follow their reporting guidelines, be transparent about how you're using funds, and stick to the mission you pitched them. You cannot just take the money and run. You're accountable to your sponsor, just like they're accountable to their donors and the IRS.

A fiscal sponsor adds credibility. Many donors and grant-makers prefer working with established nonprofits, and sponsorship gives your project legitimacy. It also takes care of tax filings, compliance, and donor receipts, all the logistical headaches that come with nonprofit fundraising. Most importantly, it allows you to focus on the work instead of getting buried in regulations.

I have used fiscal sponsors on several of my social- and environmental-impact documentaries. *A Plastic Ocean* was entirely funded by nonprofits and through fiscal sponsorships. It's a film I'm intensely proud of producing, the perfect mix of project, purpose, and aligned nonprofits.

How do I find a fiscal sponsor?

Start by identifying organizations that are in tune with your project's mission. If you're creating a community arts program, look for nonprofits in arts education. If you're working on a historical preservation project, find a nonprofit dedicated to cultural heritage. Once you have a list of potential sponsors, prepare a strong pitch. Think of it like applying for a grant. Explain your project's mission, your fundraising plan, and why their organization is the right fit. Be clear about what you need from them and what you bring to the table.

If they're interested, they'll outline the terms: administrative fees, fund management, and reporting requirements. Review everything carefully. Make sure their process aligns with how you plan to work.

And once I have one, what should I do next?

Once you're sponsored, use their credibility to your advantage. Mention them in your fundraising materials, apply for grants under their umbrella, and attend their events to expand your network. Fiscal sponsorship handles money and, even more importantly, opens doors.

And always, always stay transparent. Keep detailed records of how funds are used, follow reporting guidelines, and communicate regularly with your sponsor. Trust is the foundation of a good sponsorship, and the stronger that trust, the more opportunities you'll have down the road.

Is fiscal sponsorship right for me?

If you have a project with a clear social or cultural mission, but you're not ready to start a nonprofit, fiscal sponsorship can be a game changer. It allows you to access funding and resources while staying focused on your creative work. But if your project is a long-term one and involves multiple initiatives, and you are really serious about it, you might want to consider forming your own.

How do I set up my own nonprofit?

70

BECOMING A NONPROFIT

A nonprofit isn't merely a passion project with a good cause. It's a legal structure, a financial model, and a long-term commitment. It changes how you raise money, how you operate, and how you are held accountable. For some creative endeavors, it's the perfect fit. For others, it's an administrative headache that drains more energy than it's worth.

So, it's not just about getting funding?

Correct. A nonprofit exists to serve a mission rather than to generate profit for owners or shareholders. It can raise money through tax-deductible donations, apply for grants, and in most cases, operate tax-free. Those are big advantages. But they also mean you're not running a personal business anymore. You're running an organization that belongs to the public good. You will face intense, and appropriate, scrutiny if the major beneficiary is you.

What if I just want to get funding for a single project?

Then creating a nonprofit probably isn't the right move. If your work is temporary, primarily self-funded, or serves a personal creative goal, fiscal sponsorship (which we just talked about) or a for-profit model may be better options.

A nonprofit structure makes sense when your mission serves the public good. If your work benefits a broader community—through education, the arts, environmental advocacy, or social justice—then incorporation could be the right step. It's also a good fit if you plan to rely on donations and grants over the long term, since many funding sources are only available to nonprofits. Most importantly, if your project is meant to last, becoming a nonprofit provides structure and financial stability beyond a single funding cycle.

But if you're running a personal creative business and simply want financial stability, a nonprofit may not be the best fit. It will not be a financial panacea. Instead, the organization will own or control the assets, including your creative work, and you'll likely need to pay yourself a salary through it.

If I decide it would be right for my creative work long term, how do I actually become a nonprofit?

It starts with a single question: What is your mission? Your mission statement needs to be clear, specific, and aligned with the requirements for tax-exempt status. For example, here's the purpose statement of Next Echo Foundation, a nonprofit I started more than a dozen years ago: "The purpose of Next Echo Foundation is to nurture and empower creative and socially-engaged people and their work in order to foster a culture that is vibrant, resilient, sustaining, inclusive, diverse, self-aware, and advances toward social justice. Next Echo supports creative work and journalism that shapes our culture moving forward, and work that reflects society, so we may understand ourselves more clearly."

Once you have the foundation of a mission statement, you'll need to assemble a board of directors. Most states require at least three board members to oversee governance. Choose people who believe in your mission and bring skills like fundraising, finance, and community engagement.

Then, file Articles of Incorporation to legally establish your organization in your state. This document outlines your mission, structure, and intent to operate as a nonprofit. Once that's filed, you can apply for

501(c)(3) status with the IRS. This designation grants tax-exempt status and allows you to accept tax-deductible donations. The application process can take months and requires detailed information about your organization's activities, finances, and governance.

Beyond the legal setup, you'll need clear financial systems, fundraising structures, and operational policies. Donor management tools, accounting software, and compliance processes will become part of your daily reality.

That sounds like a lot.

It is. But for the right project, it's worth it.

Chiwan Choi, Judeth Oden Choi, and Peter Woods worked together for fifteen years. Chiwan is an editor, poet, and mentor; Judeth is a designer and technologist; Peter is a producer. Collectively they called themselves Writ Large Press, seeking to re-imagine publishing through developing and publishing authors from underserved communities. They worked under existing nonprofit umbrellas, including Next Echo's. Then, a couple of years ago, they were ready: They became their own nonprofit. Now Writ Large Foundation exists to advance the work with structured continuity.

How do I know if this is the right move for me?

Before taking the leap, ask yourself: Is my mission a sustainable long-term one? If your work is project-based or constantly evolving, incorporation might not be necessary.

Ask yourself: Do I have a team? Running a nonprofit alone is exhausting. A strong board and administrative support are essential.

Ask yourself: Am I ready for paperwork and compliance? Nonprofits must meet strict financial and legal requirements, including annual tax filings and donor reporting.

If you're uncertain, explore fiscal sponsorship first. It offers many benefits of nonprofit status without the burden of full incorporation.

What's the best way to start?

Learn from existing nonprofits in your field. Study successful organizations. What do they do well? What challenges do they face? Start small, with one program, one funding source, and scale gradually. Plan your fundraising early—grants, events, especially individual donors—so you're not constantly scrambling for resources. Investing in infrastructure for donor databases, accounting systems, and financial management tools will save you time and stress down the road.

Becoming a nonprofit is a leap of faith and a leap into structure. It transforms your creative work into a mission-driven entity capable of making lasting change. With careful planning and a clear vision, you can build an organization that amplifies your impact and creates a legacy of good.

But what if I'm not ready for all of that? Can I still raise funds for my creative work? What about crowdfunding?

71

CROWDFUNDING

You want to raise money. Of course. But crowdfunding is about so much more than that. It's about rallying a community around your work, engaging people who believe in your vision, and building momentum that can carry your project far beyond a single campaign. If you do it right, the money is just the beginning.

I thought crowdfunding was just asking people for donations.

That's the mistake a lot of creatives make. Crowdfunding is a project launch, more than a money-machine. Platforms like Kickstarter, Indiegogo, and GoFundMe have reshaped the way creative projects get made, allowing artists, filmmakers, musicians, and entrepreneurs to bypass traditional gatekeepers and go straight to the people who care most.

It works like this: You present your project, set a funding goal, and invite people to contribute. In return, backers might receive early access, exclusive content, or physical rewards. But the most valuable thing you gain is an audience.

Okay, but what if my campaign flops?

Then you've still learned something crucial: whether your idea resonates. Crowdfunding is a test. If people are willing to put money behind your project, you know you're onto something. If they aren't, you've just saved yourself months or years of chasing an idea that might not connect the way you thought.

Filmmaker Jennifer Kent didn't have enough money to finish her indie psychological horror film *The Babadook,* so she turned to Kickstarter. She raised $30,000 from 259 backers. Those 259 backers became lifelong supporters, early fans, who spread the word and fueled the movie's critical awareness and streaming success.

That's the power of crowdfunding when done right.

So what makes a campaign successful?

Storytelling. The best crowdfunding pitches make backers feel like they're part of something bigger. Why does this project matter? Why should people care? If you're funding a book, what makes it different? If you're making a film, why does this story need to be told? People back people. They want to believe in you as much as in what you're making.

Strong visuals help. A great video or compelling images do more in seconds than paragraphs of text ever will. And specificity is key. If your goal is to create a music album, don't just say "I'm making an album." Say, "This is an album about resilience, blending jazz and hip-hop influences, recorded with musicians I've worked with for years." The clearer your vision, the more confident people will feel in backing you.

How do I set the right funding goal?

One of the biggest crowdfunding mistakes? Asking for too much, too soon. People want to back something they believe will succeed. If your goal feels impossible, they may hesitate to contribute at all.

Keep your funding target practical, enough to cover your costs, but still attainable. Factor in platform fees, taxes, and the cost of fulfilling rewards. And if you have ambitious plans, consider stretch goals. Once you hit your initial target, additional goals keep the excitement going.

Wait. Rewards? What am I supposed to offer?

Backers want to support you, but they also love being part of something special. The best rewards feel personal and exclusive: early access to your work, limited-edition items, behind-the-scenes content, one-on-one experiences. A digital download of your film, a signed print, a live-streamed Q&A. These kinds of perks build a deeper connection with your audience.

What you don't want are rewards that are expensive or complicated to fulfill. If you're spending more time shipping merchandise than making your project, you've set yourself up for unnecessary stress.

What if nobody finds my campaign?

That's the biggest misconception about crowdfunding: "If I launch it, they will come." They won't. Unless you bring them in.

Crowdfunding is an event, and like any event, you have to promote it. Talk about your project early—on social media, in newsletters, in personal conversations. Build an audience before you launch. The most successful campaigns have a group of people excited and ready to pledge before Day One.

Momentum matters. Crowdfunding platforms are algorithm-driven, which means early backers increase your visibility. If you can line up people to contribute in the first forty-eight hours, your campaign is far more likely to succeed.

What are the biggest mistakes people make?

Underestimating costs: It's easy to focus on production but forget about taxes, platform fees, and reward fulfillment.

Ignoring your backers: These people aren't just customers; they're invested in your success. Keep them updated, thank them publicly, and make them feel like insiders.

Vanishing after the campaign: Whether you hit your goal or not, follow up. Show gratitude. Let people know what happens next.

What if I don't hit my goal? Is the whole thing a failure?

Probably not. Even if you don't raise what you hoped, you still gain visibility, feedback, and connections. Some campaigns that fall short still attract the attention of investors or industry professionals. Some backers may support your next project because they saw your effort. The process itself teaches valuable skills in marketing, storytelling, and audience engagement.

Okay, so should I do it?

If you're ready to put in the effort for the money, yes, but especially for the audience-building, the storytelling, and the long-term impact—then yes. Crowdfunding isn't just a way to fund a project. It's a way to build your creative future.

Yikes, you always have to work for your money! Right? Are there any other ways?

72

WHEN TO TAKE ON DEBT

Debt carries weight. It's risky. It makes people nervous. But it's not the enemy. Used wisely, it can be the key that unlocks your next step, the difference between staying where you are and breaking through. It can buy you time to finish a project, give you access to tools that elevate your work, or create an opportunity you couldn't otherwise afford. The danger lies in borrowing without a plan.

Every creative career comes with expenses. A filmmaker needs equipment. A musician might need to book studio time. A writer could benefit from stepping away from client work to finish a book. If cash flow is tight, debt can act as a bridge, connecting where you are to where you want to be. But a bridge only works if it leads somewhere. Taking on debt without a clear plan for how it will generate returns—that's when it turns from a tool into a trap.

Debt feels like a four-letter word, doesn't it?

It can be. If you borrow without a plan, it can trap you instead of freeing you. That's why the real question isn't "Should I take on debt?" It's "Does this debt serve my future?"

Smart debt funds growth. It's a business decision. It might mean upgrading to a better camera because you have clients lined up who will pay for the quality. It might mean renting a workspace because meeting clients in a coffee shop is costing you credibility. It might mean taking out a small loan to fund production costs for an album that has a real chance of selling. These are calculated moves.

When I wrote my first book, *Inside Track for Independent Filmmakers,* I decided to self-publish it. I believed in the project, believed it needed to come out now, not eighteen months from now, as legacy publishers told me. I put the cost of self-publishing on my credit card, and three weeks after the book was on sale, I'd made all that money back. It worked out for me. Probably because I spent a good chunk of the money on marketing.

That worked for you. But what about people who end up drowning in debt?

The biggest mistake creatives make with debt is borrowing based on hope instead of reality. Hope that a project will generate returns. Hope that future earnings will be enough to cover payments. Hope that things will just work out. Debt should never be a gamble. If the numbers don't add up today, they won't magically add up tomorrow.

Taking on debt is like any other creative risk. It needs to be intentional. Borrow only what you need, even if you can qualify for more. Avoid high-interest, predatory loans that drain your resources faster than you can replenish them. Invest in things that generate revenue, and avoid spending on items that just make you look or feel more professional.

So when is debt a smart move?

When it's directly tied to growth, when the risk is calculated, and when you have a concrete plan to pay it back. If it's just filling a financial gap with no clear return, don't do it.

Debt can fuel your success or bury you under stress. The difference is strategy. If you borrow with a clear purpose and a repayment plan, it becomes a stepping-stone instead of a stumbling block. And once you've got a handle on debt? The next step is knowing exactly where you stand financially. Because making smart money moves starts with understanding where you are today.

Ugh. I knew this was coming.

73

FINANCIAL SITUATIONAL AWARENESS

You can't control when inspiration strikes, but you can control whether your bank account is ready for it.

Nothing kills creativity faster than money stress. When you're constantly worried about covering rent and bills or whether you can afford to take a risk on a new project, it's hard to focus on the work itself. But financial awareness isn't about being rich. It's about knowing where you stand so you can make smart choices.

Creative careers are unpredictable. Paychecks don't arrive on a set schedule. Some months, you're flush with cash; other months, you wonder if you should start driving for a delivery app. But while creativity thrives on risk, your financial life doesn't have to. Money shouldn't be what holds you back from pursuing opportunities, experimenting with new ideas, or simply breathing easier.

So, I have to start thinking like a businessperson?

You do. Not in a soul-crushing, spreadsheet-obsessed way. Just in a way that protects your future. Most people with traditional jobs have financial structures built in: paychecks, employer contributions to taxes, maybe even a 401(k). As a creative entrepreneur, you may not. You're often your own employer, accountant, and financial strategist. That means understanding where your money comes from, where it's going, and how to make it work for you instead of against you.

I have no idea where I stand. Is that bad?

It's normal. Most creatives avoid looking at their money until they absolutely have to. But financial situational awareness means taking a step back and assessing your reality. Without fear, without judgment.

The first step is knowing your net worth. That sounds harder than it is. It's simply this: what you own minus what you owe. If your net worth is negative, don't panic. It just means you should focus on reducing debt before making big investments. The second step is tracking your cash flow. Look at the past six months. What's coming in? What's going out? What patterns do you see? If you're earning more than you spend, great—you can start investing in tools, education, or savings. If you're spending more than you earn, it's time to rethink unnecessary expenses before they become a crisis.

Okay, but what about saving? That feels impossible.

It just needs to be built into your system. An emergency fund gives you options. It lets you walk away from bad clients, fund your own passion projects, and take risks without financial panic. Aim for six to eighteen months of essential expenses saved up, but don't let the number intimidate you. Start small. Even setting aside 5 to 10 percent of each payment builds over time.

What if I'm not even sure where to start?

Simplify. Separate your accounts. Keep business and personal finances distinct. Automate savings, even if it's a small amount. And set aside taxes immediately, because if you're self-employed, no one is withholding for you. The worst feeling in the world is a tax bill you weren't prepared for. Treat it like rent: money you never touch.

Financial awareness isn't about being rich. It's about being informed. When you know where you stand, you make smarter decisions. You reduce stress. You gain control over your creative career.

And once you have a clear picture of your finances, the next step is making your money work harder for you.

I just want to focus on my work. I hate thinking about money.

74

NO ONE WILL TAKE CARE OF YOUR MONEY BETTER THAN YOU

If you don't take care of your money, someone else will. And not always in your best interest.

The history of art is filled with horror stories of brilliant creatives who lost everything because they trusted the wrong people, didn't pay attention, or assumed someone else "had it handled." You don't have to be one of them. Financial vigilance isn't about greed. It's about freedom. It's about making sure you can keep doing your work on your own terms, without panic, without regret, without the gut-wrenching realization that your years of effort have been siphoned away.

But I have a business manager. They handle everything.

That's what Leonard Cohen thought, too.

Cohen, the poet and musician, trusted his longtime manager with his finances. By the time he realized she had stolen over $5 million from his retirement fund, most of it was gone. He won a legal battle—but that didn't bring his money back. Instead, he was forced to tour extensively in his seventies to rebuild his finances.

Billy Joel? Same story. His manager, who was also his brother-in-law, misused his funds, costing him millions. And these are just the famous ones. For every Leonard Cohen or Billy Joel, there are thousands of lesser-known creatives who wake up one day to find their accounts empty, their taxes unpaid, their futures in ruins.

That's terrifying. So what am I supposed to do?

You don't need to become a financial expert. You just need basic awareness and the habit of checking in. First, get comfortable with financial basics. Budgeting, taxes, investing are not optional. Know how much you earn, how much you spend, and what you owe. Track it, even if it's just a quick glance at your bank accounts every week. If you don't know where your money is going, you're already losing control.

Second, monitor your accounts. Even if you hire professionals, always check your bank statements, investment accounts, and credit cards. Fraud happens. Mistakes happen. People you trust make bad decisions. Set a calendar reminder to do a fifteen-minute financial check-in every month.

Third, if you want to or need to, hire the right people, but stay involved. Vet accountants, business managers, and financial advisors thoroughly. Look for people who understand creatives and are working with people at the same point in their careers as you. Demand transparency. If someone is vague about where your money is, that's a red flag. Retain control. Never give one person unchecked access to your accounts or decision-making power. You should always have the final say. Personally approve every payment that goes out.

But I don't even like dealing with money. Isn't that what financial managers are for?

Your financial health is like your physical health. You don't have to be a doctor, but you still need to know when something feels off, when to ask questions, and when to get a second opinion. Even if you trust your financial team, get an independent review once a year. A forensic accountant can spot irregularities before they become disasters.

What about investments? I hear about people getting rich off crypto, start-ups, and stocks.

Maybe. But before you throw your money into something trendy, ask yourself: Do I understand this investment? If you can't explain it to a friend, don't put your money in it. Ask: Is this money I can afford to lose? Never invest what you can't part with. Ask: Does this align with my long-term goals? Investing in something just because it sounds lucrative is a great way to lose money fast. Avoid anything that feels secretive, too good to be true, or dependent on someone else's charisma.

Taking charge of your finances will build your confidence in your decisions. When you know where your money is, you don't panic when unexpected expenses hit. When you track your earnings, you can say "no" to lowball offers without fear. When you set up financial guardrails, you can take creative risks without financial ruin lurking around the corner.

What if I've already made mistakes?

Then you start now. Awareness is power. No matter where you are financially, today is better than tomorrow when it comes to taking control.

Your art is your legacy. Your finances sustain it. No matter how successful you become or how many professionals you hire, you are the ultimate authority on your money. Stay informed. Stay engaged. And make sure that the only person making creative and financial decisions for you is you.

Okay, but how should I make those decisions?

75

INVEST CONSERVATIVELY

I thought investing was supposed to be exciting. Aren't I supposed to be chasing big wins?

That's a myth. Your creative career already carries enough risk. The passion projects, the unpredictable paychecks, the long stretches between gigs. Your investments? They should be the opposite: stable, steady, and boring. Think of your finances as the ground beneath you, solid enough that you can take creative leaps without worrying about crashing.

So investing isn't about getting rich overnight?

No. Investing is about freedom.

Freedom to choose projects so you're not forced to take uninspiring work just to pay the bills. Freedom from panic so you can survive income gaps without stress. Freedom to pivot so you have the resources to pursue opportunities, start new ventures, or take time off to recharge.

High-risk investments are tempting. Who doesn't want to double their money fast? But for creatives, losing money on a bad bet can set you back years. Take Oprah Winfrey. Early in her career, she lived frugally, saved aggressively, and avoided high-risk financial moves. That financial cushion let her focus on her craft and her long-term business ambitions. Her investments weren't flashy, but they gave her the basic stability she needed to start building her media empire.

Okay, how do I actually invest conservatively?

First, build your foundation. Before you invest a single dollar, secure your essentials: an emergency fund of six to twelve months of living expenses in a high-yield savings account and a consistent, realistic budget for investing. Never invest money you might need next month.

Next, stick to low-risk, reliable investments. Index funds and ETFs provide instant diversification with steady growth. Bonds offer predictable returns. Target-date funds automatically shift toward safer assets as you age. These aren't exciting, but they work.

Does my age change how I should invest?

Yes. Early in your career, focus on long-term growth, allocating more to stocks. As you get older, shift toward protecting what you've built with more bonds and dividend-paying investments. The closer you are to needing the money, the safer your portfolio should be.

The real key is consistency. Automate contributions to your investment account so you're growing wealth even when you're focused on your work. Avoid high-fee financial products that eat away at returns. Be patient, stay the course. Markets fluctuate, but conservative investing is about the long game.

So I'm never supposed to take risks?

Calculated risks, yes. But the risks should be in your creative work. Your investments should create a safety net.

Your money should work for you, not stress you out. By building a solid, conservative investment plan, you create the stability that lets you take risks where you should: in your art, your business, your career.

Some months, I feel like a millionaire. Other months, I'm living on Cup o' Ramen. What can I do?

76

SAVE MONEY FOR YOUR LUMPY INCOME AND YOUR FUTURE

Welcome to the reality of lumpy income, a financial rhythm that's unpredictable, exhilarating, and sometimes terrifying. One month, you're flooded with paychecks; the next, it's a drought. That's why saving is a creative survival skill.

But saving isn't just about covering the dry spells. It's about securing your future, ensuring that when your career evolves, slows down, or takes an unexpected turn, you're financially prepared. The way you save today determines the choices you'll have tomorrow.

So I need an emergency fund?

Yes, but not just an emergency fund. You need a lumpy income buffer and a future-proof savings strategy.

Most financial advice suggests saving three to six months of expenses. That works for salaried workers, but creatives need six to twelve months. It's about your creative freedom. A solid buffer gives you breathing room between projects and lets you take control of your career instead of reacting to financial pressure. As a producer, I will work on multiple projects for years, for free, in the hope of one getting made.

When a film is produced, yes, there's a payday, but I sock most it away so I can afford to wait until the next film is made.

But I barely know what next month looks like. How am I supposed to plan for the next ten years?

That's exactly why you need to save. The future is coming whether you're ready or not. Your career will evolve, markets will change, unexpected life events will happen. The more you prepare now, the more freedom you'll have later.

Savings give you options. They let you walk away from bad deals, invest in your own projects, and survive the curveballs of life.

So, how much should I actually be saving?

During high-earning years, aim to save 20 to 30 percent of your income. Windfalls won't last forever; act like they won't. I have known many people who got a big payday, assumed it would be repeated every year, and spent large. That rarely works out well.

Start with an emergency fund of six to twelve months of expenses in a high-yield savings account. Contribute the maximum to retirement accounts like IRAs or Solo 401(k)s for long-term security and tax benefits.

That sounds like a lot.

It does, but it's about consistency. Small contributions add up over time. The more you save now, the more creative control you'll have later.

Saving is about empowering your future. Whether you're smoothing out the highs and lows of your income or securing financial independence for decades to come, the decisions you make today will define the choices you have tomorrow.

How does all this impact my taxes?

77

GET YOUR TAX DEDUCTIONS

Taxes aren't just an obligation, they're an opportunity. Every dollar you spend on your creative work could be a dollar that lowers your taxable income. If you know how to claim it.

I know I need to understand taxes, but... Ugh. I'd rather spend my time creating.

I hear you.

Think of tax deductions as your financial safety net. The more you take advantage of them, the more money stays in your pocket to reinvest in your art, your business, and your future. But to do it right, you need to understand what's deductible, keep clean records, and always stay on the right side of the law.

Unlike salaried workers, most creatives don't have an employer withholding taxes from their paycheck. That means when tax season rolls around, you could owe a hefty sum unless you've reduced your taxable income by claiming legitimate business expenses.

Wait, so I can write off my new laptop?

If you use it primarily for work, yes. But knowing what qualifies and keeping proper documentation is what keeps you safe from audits and financial headaches.

If you're a freelancer or independent creative, many of your daily business expenses can be deducted. Your workspace, whether a dedicated home office or a co-working space, is partially deductible. The tools of your trade—software, hardware, and materials—are all eligible. Reasonable and necessary travel for work, marketing expenses, professional services (lawyers, accountants, assistants), and industry-related training can also lower your taxable income.

But there are limits. Your personal Netflix subscription? Not deductible. A designer outfit that makes you feel confident in meetings? Unless it's a required costume, the IRS says no. Deduct only what is *directly* related to your work.

Stay organized to stay audit-proof, or at least be able to glide through an audit if the IRS comes calling. Separate your business and personal finances. Open a dedicated business bank account and credit card, and use them exclusively for work-related expenses. Track every dollar coming in and out. If you drive for work, log your miles. If you claim a home office, be precise: Measure your space and calculate the percentage of your home it occupies.

Okay, but what about actually filing my taxes?

That's where freelancers have extra responsibilities. When you're self-employed, you're running a business. No one is withholding taxes for you, so you have to set them aside and pay them yourself. On top of income tax, you owe self-employment tax, which covers Social Security and Medicare. If you expect to owe more than $1,000 in taxes, you must make estimated payments quarterly.

Wait, quarterly taxes? No one told me about that.

Yeah, a lot of freelancers get hit with a nasty surprise their first year. If you don't make estimated payments, you could owe penalties when tax season arrives.

To avoid a disaster, save 25 to 30 percent of every payment you receive. Try this: Open a separate savings account just for taxes and transfer money into it as soon as you get paid.

What forms do I need?

In the United States, you'll typically file:

Schedule C—Reports your income and expenses.
Schedule SE—Calculates your self-employment tax.
Form 1040—Your main tax return.
Form 1099-NEC—If a client paid you over $600, they'll send you this form. Even if they don't, you still have to report the income.

If you live outside the United States, tax laws vary widely. If you work internationally, you may need to file taxes in multiple countries or navigate treaties that prevent double taxation. If you're unsure, get professional advice.

Susie, a graphic illustrator I know, learned the hard way. Her first year as a freelancer, she didn't set aside money for taxes and didn't make quarterly payments. By April, she owed thousands plus penalties. It took her two years to recover. The next year, she worked with an accountant, automated her tax savings, and paid quarterly. The result? No stress, no panic, and financial stability.

I hate to ask for this, but break it down for me. Can I have a checklist?

Track all income and expenses. Keep invoices, receipts, and records.

Set aside tax money from every payment. Automate it if possible.

Know your tax deadlines. Mark quarterly due dates on your calendar.

Consider working with a tax pro. They can find deductions you missed and help you avoid penalties.

Taxes aren't anyone person's favorite subject, except my accountant, who loves them, God bless her. For the rest of us, handling taxes right protects our careers. Stay organized, plan ahead, and treat your freelance work like the business it is.

Okay. Can we get back to that business? How do I actually get my work out there?

78

HUMANS RELATE TO HUMANS: NETWORKING AND PROFESSIONAL COMMUNICATIONS

What if I told you that your next big break isn't about how talented you are, but about who knows you exist?

That sounds unfair.

It does, but it's the reality of creative careers. No matter how brilliant your work, how unique your vision, or how polished your portfolio, success doesn't happen in isolation. People hire people they trust, recommend creatives they like, and champion projects they feel connected to. Your craft might open the door, but it's your relationships that keep you in the room. And how you communicate? That determines whether you're remembered, respected, and recommended or ignored.

I just want my work to speak for itself.

It will, to a point. But relationships drive careers. The best opportunities don't always go to the most talented person; they go to the person who knows how to engage others with professionalism, clarity, and respect. Every email, message, or conversation you have shapes how people perceive you as an artist, and as someone they want to work with. Respect builds trust. Clear, concise, and considerate communication shows that you value people's time. Your words shape your reputation. Whether you're pitching a project, reaching out to a mentor, or discussing collaboration, how you communicate determines whether people champion your work—or forget about it.

I hate networking. It feels fake.

That's because you're thinking about it the wrong way. Networking isn't about pushing yourself on others. It is about building relationships. The best networkers aren't the loudest self-promoters; they're the ones who listen, who show genuine interest, and who contribute before they ask for anything. It's not about handing out business cards like confetti or cold-pitching strangers. It's about making real connections. Forget the transactional mindset. Approach networking the way you approach your creative work—with curiosity, openness, and a desire to connect.

Start with your inner circle. Your strongest network is already around you: friends, colleagues, mentors, former collaborators. Tell them what you're working on. Share your goals. They might know someone who needs exactly what you offer. Show up where your people are. Attend industry events, meetups, and workshops. Instead of worrying about "networking," focus on having good conversations. Ask people about their work. Listen. Let connections happen naturally. Engage online with purpose. Follow people whose work inspires you, comment thoughtfully, and send direct messages when you genuinely appreciate someone's work without immediately asking for anything. Be a connector, not just a seeker. Introduce two people who might collaborate well together. Recommend a resource, book, or tool that might help someone. Support other creatives by sharing their work. When you focus on giving, people naturally want to help you in return. Follow up and stay in touch. Most connections fade because people don't follow up.

A simple message like "Great meeting you last week. Really enjoyed our conversation about storytelling! Hope to stay in touch." can turn a one-time meeting into a long-term relationship.

But what if I don't know where to start?

Think of networking as part of your craft. Set small goals: Meet one new person at every event, send one thoughtful message a week. Make it a habit. Long-term relationships matter more than quick connections. Lin-Manuel Miranda didn't build *Hamilton* alone. Before becoming a global phenomenon, he steadily built his network in the Broadway world, collaborating with peers, attending workshops, and staying in close contact with mentors like Stephen Sondheim. His relationships helped bring *Hamilton* to life and ensured its early champions were people he trusted. Miranda's success has been driven by meaningful, sustained connections.

Is it okay to text someone about a job opportunity? Should I DM a producer on Instagram? What if my email goes unanswered?

Different platforms demand different levels of formality. Knowing which to use, and how to use them, can make or break a connection. Email is still the most professional way to reach out. Use a clear subject line, a polite greeting, and get to the point quickly. Keep it short; people skim emails. Close with a call to action. If you want a meeting, ask for it: "Would you be open to a quick call next week?" Avoid long, rambling messages, too many exclamation points, and attachments with no explanation. But also know: Emails are a flood-zone and people may not see them, so it's okay to resend the same email after a few days.

Text messaging works best for quick confirmations or informal check-ins, not detailed discussions. Keep messages short, professional, and sent at appropriate hours. Social media can be a great networking tool if you use it thoughtfully. Engage before you message. Comment on someone's work before sliding into their DMs. If you reach out, be direct but respectful: "Hi [Name], I love your work on [specific project]. If you're open to it, I'd love to connect and learn more about your process."

What about in-person meetings?

In-person conversations leave a lasting impression. Introduce yourself with confidence but warmth. A simple "Hi, I'm [Your Name]. I really admire your work on [project]" goes a long way. Be interested, not just interesting. Bring a business card or portfolio if it's appropriate, but don't overwhelm people with self-promotion. Good networking is about listening as much as speaking. Ava DuVernay built her career not by aggressively pitching herself, but by asking insightful questions, listening intently, and following up with thoughtful thank-you notes. She understood that relationships aren't built overnight, they're cultivated over time.

What if I make a mistake?

Mistakes happen. Maybe you send an awkward email. Maybe you fumble through a conversation. The key is to learn and adjust. The more you practice professional communication, the more natural it becomes. Networking isn't a one-time task. It's an ongoing process. Relationships take time to develop, and the strongest ones come from consistency, generosity, and authenticity.

Your creative career is built on more than talent. It's built on trust. The way you communicate today shapes the opportunities you get tomorrow. Stay professional, be thoughtful, and invest in relationships the same way you invest in your craft. Humans relate to humans, and in the creative world, relationships are everything.

Isn't my work enough? If I'm great at what I do, won't people just notice?

79

SOCIAL RULES AND PATHWAYS FOR CREATIVE CAREERS

Talent alone doesn't guarantee success. Creative fields aren't meritocracies. They're ecosystems. Each industry has its own rhythms, unspoken rules, and gatekeepers. The way opportunities arise, careers develop, and reputations are built varies depending on the field you're in. Understanding these differences helps you play the long game, avoid unnecessary frustration, and make strategic choices about your future.

I don't want to play by someone else's rules.

You don't have to. But knowing the terrain means you can decide when to follow the path, when to step off it, and when to carve your own. The art world moves differently from the music industry. Publishing has different gatekeepers than film has. The expectations, timelines, and relationships that shape each field are just as important as the work itself. Who you know matters, not in a shallow, transactional way, but because creative industries are built on trust, recommendations, and collaborations. Some fields reward early success, while others favor slow-building reputations. Knowing how careers typically unfold in your industry helps you pace yourself, embrace reinvention, and avoid burnout.

A visual artist's career often unfolds slowly, with relationships to curators, collectors, and institutions determining success. Unlike industries that prize youth, many artists reach their peak later in life, after years of critical recognition. Music careers tend to be built on early momentum—viral moments, industry backing, or relentless gigging. Then their longevity requires reinvention. Theater careers take years to build, often centered on close relationships between directors, playwrights, dramaturgs, and artistic directors. Film and media are deeply collaborative; most careers begin with assistant roles or indie projects before breaking into larger productions. Graphic design and fashion rely on portfolios, with designers often freelancing or assisting before launching independent brands. Writers endure long roads of rejection, often starting in short-form media before breaking into books or screenplays. Photography blends artistic storytelling with commercial viability, with careers often built on a mix of freelance work, personal projects, and industry recognition. AI engineers and designers can rise like rockets, because it is a new industry, but as AI becomes commonplace their career-paths will move into more familiar trajectories.

This all sounds great, but how do I apply it to my own career?

Study how successful creatives in your field built their careers. Look for patterns. Where did they start? Who did they collaborate with? What risks did they take? Adapt to your industry's social rules. If your field thrives on networking, show up at the right events: hackathons, gallery openings, film festivals, book fairs, fashion weeks. Engage with the community both online and offline. If an industry values formal mentorship, find someone to guide you. If it's more of a DIY, self-made space, start building and putting your work out independently. Follow industry norms for how work is shared, presented, and discussed.

Pace yourself for longevity. If your field rewards early success, seize opportunities quickly. If it values experience and depth, don't rush. Build consistently and let your reputation grow over time. Longevity isn't just about avoiding burnout; it's about knowing the rhythm of your industry and adjusting accordingly.

Barry Jenkins didn't arrive at *Moonlight* overnight. He started with a tiny indie film, *Medicine for Melancholy*, which earned critical praise but limited recognition. He spent years working behind the scenes before his breakthrough. His journey shows the power of persistence and how relationships within the indie film world led to opportunities that shaped his career.

Your creative career isn't built on talent alone. It's built on trust. The way you communicate today shapes the opportunities you get tomorrow. Stay professional, be thoughtful, and invest in relationships the same way you invest in your craft. Creative careers don't follow a single path, yet they all have social rules, hidden expectations, and unwritten maps that guide them. The more you understand the landscape of your industry, the better you can navigate it. You can't follow someone else's path, just as you can't step into the same river. But by making informed, intentional choices you will forge your own journey.

And that journey will be my creative career?

80

SCAFFOLDING YOUR CAREERS (YOU WILL HAVE EIGHT CAREERS)

Wait… eight careers? That sounds exhausting.

Actually, it's freeing. The myth of the "one career for life" is long gone, especially for creatives. The most successful artists, writers, musicians, filmmakers, and designers don't follow a single, uninterrupted trajectory. They move through cycles, building, mastering, pivoting, reinventing. Each career you create won't erase the last; it will add to it, strengthening the structure that supports your life's work.

There will be a moment when everything stops. The network cancels your show. The editor who championed your work moves on. The industry shifts, and suddenly, you're on the outside looking in. Every creative career, no matter how successful, eventually confronts the empty space—that unsettling pause when the momentum you've built vanishes overnight.

This is the moment that defines you. Some people take it as a sign to leave, to step away from the uncertainty and find something more stable. Others—those who build long, enduring creative lives—push through. They don't wait for the industry to invite them back. They pivot, adapt, reinvent themselves to find solid ground again.

The ones who make it through understand this core truth: Creativity is a business. It is not only about talent, inspiration, or even hard work. Like any start-up, it is primarily about sustainability. To survive the empty space, you need to know how to run yourself like a business.

Here's the essential element of persistence: Reinvention is a strategy.

But what if I don't want to change careers that many times?

You don't have to force it. Change will happen naturally, sometimes as an opportunity, sometimes as a necessity. The goal isn't to stay in one lane forever. It's to build a structure strong enough to let you move freely between them. The projects that excite you at age 25 won't be the same ones that fulfill you at age 50. The world will shift around you. Technology evolves, industries rise and fall, economic and cultural forces reshape creative opportunities. You will outgrow some things, and that's a good thing. Each career prepares you for what's next, even if you don't see it at the time.

Your first career will be about finding your voice. The aspiring creative phase is when you're figuring it out, experimenting, working on passion projects, learning your craft, absorbing influences, and seeking your creative identity. You're likely juggling other jobs to support yourself, making little (or no) money from your work yet. But this phase is where your foundation takes shape. Think of a filmmaker working as a production assistant while shooting short films on weekends. Then comes your emerging professional phase, the moment you start getting paid. Maybe not much, maybe inconsistently, but you're officially working in your field. Clients, editors, curators, or collaborators begin to take notice. You say "yes" to almost everything because you're hungry for experience and credibility. This is the hustle stage, learning how to navigate the industry, make connections, and build momentum. A graphic designer freelancing for small clients while building a brand on social media.

Then you refine. The specialized creator phase is when you stop saying yes to everything and start shaping your career with intention. You become known for something: a particular style, a skill set, a niche.

Your work gains traction, and opportunities become more consistent. A songwriter who has become the go-to collaborator for a specific genre or artist. Then comes the first pivot point. Something shifts. Maybe your interests evolve, or the market changes, or you burn out on your current path. This is your first major reinvention, a moment where you take everything you've learned and apply it in a new way. It can feel like starting over, but you're not. You're building on what you already know. A journalist who transitions into podcast production as digital media grows.

At some point, you become an established expert. By now, you're a known name in your field. Work comes to you. You've built a network that supports and sustains you. Maybe you start mentoring others, expanding your creative business, or diversifying your income streams. This phase brings a sense of authority and stability, along with the challenge of staying relevant and inspired. A photographer who now teaches workshops and publishes books on their craft. Then another shift. The second act. Something big changes. It could be personal—family, health, a new life priority—or external, like a major industry shift. You embrace a new creative direction, not from necessity, but because you choose to. This is when many creatives return to passion projects or take their work in a deeper, more meaningful direction. A film director who pivots to nonprofit work, making documentaries that align with social causes.

Eventually, you think beyond yourself. The legacy-builder phase is when you want to create something that lasts, mentoring the next generation, shaping the culture of your field, building an institution, or cementing your influence. This phase is about contribution, not competition. A novelist who starts a residency program for emerging writers. A producer who becomes professional faculty at a university.

Then comes the final phase: the elder visionary. Your scaffolding is complete. The careers you built support you, even if you're no longer actively producing work. You've created a lasting impact, whether through royalties, intellectual property, businesses, or students who carry your work forward. Your focus shifts from creating to reflecting, teaching, and enjoying the life you've built. A painter hosting retrospectives and living off licensing deals from a lifetime of work.

This sounds like a lot of reinvention. How do I know when to pivot?

Revisit your values regularly. What matters to you now? Let that guide your choices. Seek mentors who've been through transitions; their perspective can be invaluable when you're at a crossroads. Experiment before committing. Test out new directions with small projects before fully shifting gears. Every pivot, every reinvention, every shift adds to your creative life. The strongest creative careers are flexible, adaptable, built layer by layer to withstand whatever comes next.

Yo-Yo Ma didn't have just one career. He built a scaffolding of many. He started as a classical prodigy, mastering his instrument in the traditional sense. Then he branched out, exploring jazz, Appalachian folk, and global music through his Silk Road Ensemble. He used his influence to support arts education and cultural diplomacy, expanding his impact beyond performance. Each phase built on the last, ensuring his career remained vibrant and relevant for decades. He didn't stay in one lane. He built a superhighway system.

So you're saying I'm always a start-up?

Exactly. No matter how long you've been in the game, you're always evolving, always learning, always building toward the next thing. Every career phase scaffolds onto the last, creating your stronger, richer, more resilient self.

Your creative life is a growing, evolving structure. Each career adds a new layer of strength, depth, and possibility. Change is the essential that keeps your work alive.

But really, this seems a lot. How many hats do I have to wear here?

81

YOU ARE THE CEO OF YOU

You already wear many hats: artist, dreamer, problem-solver, strategist. Whether or not you realize it, every choice you make—how you spend your time, what projects you pursue, whom you collaborate with—is a strategic decision. You may not have a corporate office or a team of employees, but you do have a business, and that business is you. Your job is to run it well.

Do I really have to think of myself as a CEO?

Yeah, you do. If you want your creativity to sustain you—financially, emotionally, and spiritually—then leading yourself with the mindset of a CEO isn't an obligation. It's a power move.

If people tell you that creativity and structure can't mix, don't believe them. Every great creative career has a scaffolding underneath it. That scaffolding isn't about rigidity; it's about leadership. A business doesn't just survive on inspiration; it needs direction, decision-making, and discipline. The same applies to your creative life. If you don't take control of it, someone else will, whether that's an exploitative contract, a manager who doesn't have your best interests at heart, or simply the inertia of saying "yes" to the wrong things.

To be a successful creative, you need to balance vision with execution. You need to lead yourself in three key ways: Businesswise—managing your career like an enterprise, making informed financial and strategic choices. Emotionally—cultivating resilience, avoiding burnout, and staying engaged with your work. Spiritually—aligning your creative work with your deeper purpose so you never feel lost in the process.

I'm not good with numbers. I just want to focus on my art.

That's exactly why you need a plan. No CEO knows everything. They just know what matters, and they build systems to keep track of the rest. Establish your vision. Every great business has a mission statement. So should you. What do you create? Why does it matter? Who is it for? Write it down.

Master the numbers. Know what you earn, what you spend, and what you need to keep going. Use a spreadsheet, an app, anything that gives you clarity. Market with authenticity. You don't have to be a social media influencer, but you do need to share your work with intention. Whether through Instagram, an email newsletter, or networking, how you present yourself matters. Set strategic goals. Think in timelines. Where do you want to be in six months? A year? Break it down into manageable steps. A creative business isn't built on talent alone—it's built on decisions. Make yours with intention.

I can handle the business side. It's the self-doubt that gets me.

That's because creativity requires vulnerability. And vulnerability requires emotional leadership. Cultivate resilience. Setbacks aren't failures; they're part of the process. Every rejection, every stalled project, every moment of doubt: These are just stepping-stones. Learn to see them that way. Practice self-compassion. Your work will never be perfect. No one's is. What matters is progress. Give yourself credit not just for finished pieces but for the steps you take.

Build a support network. Surround yourself with people who challenge and uplift you. Find mentors. Stay close to collaborators who make you better. Creative work is hard enough. Don't go it alone. A CEO's primary job is to manage people. In your case, the person you're leading is you. Treat yourself with the same patience, strategy, and care you'd offer to any other professional.

What if I lose my sense of direction?

You will. Everyone does. That's why you need something deeper than a business plan. You need a Why. Reconnect with your purpose. Regularly revisit why you create. Who are you making work for? What do you hope to leave behind? Keep asking these questions. Embrace lifelong growth. You are never "done" as an artist. There is no final version of you. Every challenge, every shift, every evolution is an opportunity to go deeper. Give back. Leadership isn't just about personal success. Mentor others. Teach. Support causes that align with your values. The best creative lives aren't just about you. They're about impact.

When Patrick Ta built his brand, Patrick Ta Beauty, he wasn't just the makeup artist. He became the CEO of a creative empire. He became an executive, shaping the details of the products, marketing, and collaborations, and led the relationships with investors, partners, and his team. Beyond the strategy, Ta led with his personal story of persistence, turning it into a vision of beauty that celebrates individuality and confidence. His creative leadership advanced his reputation and his revenues.

Thinking like a CEO doesn't mean you have to be rigid, corporate, or disconnected from your art. It means leading yourself with clarity and intention. Planning for the long term. What does sustainability look like for you? How can you make sure your work keeps supporting you—not just financially, but emotionally and creatively? Stay adaptable. Every creative career evolves. Don't cling to what worked five years ago if it's no longer serving you. Keep learning, keep shifting. Prioritize self-care. Success means nothing if you burn out before you can enjoy it. Balance ambition with rest.

So, I have to be the CEO, the artist, the marketer, the everything?

Just create. Create your strategic choices, create your resilience against the ups and downs, create your deep connection to why you create in the first place.

You are more than an artist. You are a leader. By stepping into the role of CEO of your creative life, you take control of your vision, your choices, and your future. Lead with strategy, resilience, and purpose, and you'll create extraordinary work and an extraordinary life. The power is yours.

PART THREE

THE TEN LAWS OF CULTURENOMICS

Just as you, as a creative person, fuse art and commerce, so does your work when it achieves measures of success.

Over my decades in the creative industries—spanning theater, film, music, design, entrepreneurship, education—I began to notice that there are common elements that surround creatively and financially enduring works.

Why does this happen again and again, I wondered. Do these principles truly forecast how a creative work will be received by the world? The more I observed and learned, the more apparent these principles became. A few years ago, I started to codify them. I realized that they are more than principles—they form a kind of charter for the creative and economic order of things.

Even knowing these elements exist, it is quite difficult to achieve them all. But knowing that they exist may make it easier to strive for them.

I have assembled these principles as Ten Laws of Culturenomics.

82

LAW ONE: PASSION IS THE PRIMARY UNIT OF CULTURAL VALUE

Passion is the currency that fuels cultural change. More than money, prestige, or access, it is the authentic enthusiasm of creators and audiences that determines which ideas thrive and resonate in society. Creative culture is built not by what is merely consumed but by what people deeply care about and are willing to champion. Passion is the first law of culturenomics because it underpins every subsequent force in the intersection of creativity and commerce.

Passion works as a differentiator in a world saturated with creative output. People respond to genuine enthusiasm, recognizing when a creator is deeply invested in their work. Authenticity has an unmistakable power, cutting through the noise of manufactured trends and fleeting popularity. It imbues work with a magnetic force, drawing in audiences not because they are marketed to but because they feel the sincerity of the creator's intent. The works that resonate most deeply are those that carry this intangible yet unmistakable energy.

Beyond the individual creator, passion has a connective quality. It draws like-minded individuals together, forming communities that amplify and sustain cultural movements. A single spark of enthusiasm can ripple outward, transforming personal investment into collective momentum. These communities not only champion creative efforts but also sustain them, evolving into ecosystems of shared purpose and loyalty. Passion is the seed from which movements grow, the invisible thread that binds creators to audiences and audiences to each other.

Cultural movements often meet resistance. Whether from institutions guarding the status quo or societal norms slow to embrace change, these barriers can stifle progress. But passion provides the energy and persistence needed to weather these challenges. It fortifies creators, turning obstacles into opportunities for reinvention and growth. The resilience born of passion is what enables creative work to endure skepticism, rejection, or apathy, and emerge stronger on the other side. Without passion, even technically excellent work lacks the emotional resonance to inspire devotion or catalyze change. Passion is both the fuel and the fire of cultural impact.

Consider the Impressionist movement as a vivid example of passion's transformative power. In the nineteenth century, Claude Monet, Edgar Degas, and their peers faced relentless rejection from the Paris Salon, which dismissed their work as unfinished and vulgar. Yet their passion for capturing the ephemeral beauty of light and everyday life drove them to organize their own exhibitions. Over time, their dedication reshaped public taste and permanently altered art history. Had they bowed to resistance or lacked the passion to persevere, their vision would have remained buried beneath the weight of convention. The Impressionists didn't just create; they ignited a cultural shift, fueled by their unwavering commitment to their art.

A more contemporary example is the meteoric rise of K-pop, epitomized by groups like BTS. Their global success isn't just the result of polished performances; it stems from an unparalleled emotional connection with their fans, known as ARMY. These fans embody the power of passion-driven community formation, organizing global events, sharing content, and advocating for their favorite artists in ways that defy the traditional boundaries of fandom. K-pop's global influence is a testament to how passion transforms audiences into active participants, amplifying cultural value far beyond the initial spark.

For creatives, the takeaway is clear. Passion must guide your work. Begin by identifying what you love most deeply and let that enthusiasm shape your projects and decisions. Authentic passion draws others who share your vision. Share your excitement openly, whether through social media, blogs, or in-person events. Passion is infectious, and your willingness to express it galvanizes others. Seek out or build communities around shared interests; these spaces amplify cultural momentum and provide support during challenges.

When resistance arises, and it always does, let your passion sustain you. Most groundbreaking cultural contributions faced skepticism at first. Your passion equips you to persist and adapt, transforming challenges into stepping-stones. Equally important, celebrate the passions of others. Championing the work of your peers fosters a culture of mutual inspiration and growth, creating an ecosystem where creativity thrives.

Passion isn't just a personal motivator; it is the lifeblood of cultural value. When you channel your enthusiasm into your work and connect with others who share that spark, you ignite movements that transcend individual effort. Passion changes minds, reshapes communities, and leaves an indelible imprint on the world. Lead with what you love, and others will follow.

83

LAW TWO: THE LAUNCH IS THE CONTEXT

The way your creative work is introduced to the world shapes how it is perceived, valued, and remembered. The launch is not just a moment. It is the first story told about your work. The context of where, when, how, and by whom your work is introduced becomes inseparable from the audience's experience of it. To master culturenomics, you must understand that the launch isn't merely logistical; it's a narrative act, a profound act of birth.

The first encounter audiences have with a creative work leaves a permanent impression. Whether it's the hushed reverence of a gallery opening, the electric excitement of a film premiere, or the immediacy of a social media drop, these moments frame how your audience experiences the work. Expectations, emotions, and even future interpretations are forged in that first impression. A launch is an active act of storytelling.

Timing, too, is essential. Creative works launched in alignment with cultural or societal moments can resonate far beyond their intrinsic qualities. A timely release harnesses the collective energy of a moment, embedding your work in the consciousness of its time. Conversely, a mistimed launch, whether too early, too late, or in a period of cultural distraction, can bury even the most brilliant work. The trajectory of creative success often hinges on the precision of timing.

Where your work is first presented carries its own weight of meaning. The Sistine Chapel ceiling, for example, was not simply an extraordinary artistic achievement; it was launched in a setting of profound cultural and spiritual significance. Completed in 1512 and unveiled within the Vatican, the location framed Michelangelo's work as divine revelation. This context was as important to its impact as the frescoes themselves. Art introduced in such a space becomes part of its environment, inseparable from the meanings that environment imposes.

More recently, Beyoncé's release of *Lemonade* provides a masterclass in contextualizing a launch. Debuting as a surprise visual album on HBO, it was not merely music but a cultural event. The secrecy of the launch, the integration of film, and the alignment with themes of personal and societal upheaval framed *Lemonade* as groundbreaking before a single note was played. The launch became part of the art, shaping its reception and ensuring its place as a defining cultural moment.

The context of a launch also draws power from those who champion it. Gatekeepers, influencers, and advocates wield significant influence. A collaborator or venue with cultural credibility extends that credibility to the work itself, opening doors to audiences who might not otherwise engage. This dynamic, however, requires alignment. Collaborators must authentically reflect the values and tone of the work. The wrong association can undermine even the strongest creative effort.

The launch of your work is not a separate task; it is an integral part of the work itself. Plan your launch context with the same care and intention you bring to creation. Consider the environment, the timing, and the audience's first experience. If your work carries themes of innovation, launch in a setting that embodies the future; if it explores intimacy, choose a venue or platform that fosters closeness and quiet reflection. The context becomes part of the narrative.

The launch of creative work is not an afterthought; it is a deliberate act of framing, a first impression that echoes through time. By crafting a thoughtful and strategic context, you elevate your work, ensuring it reaches the right audience in the right way. The story of your work begins with how you choose to share it. Make that story as compelling as the work itself.

84

LAW THREE: THE NARRATIVE OF CREATION IS AS IMPORTANT AS THE NARRATIVE THAT IS CREATED

When audiences engage with creative work, they're drawn not only to the finished piece but also to the story behind it. How it was made, why it was made, and who made it are narratives that deepen the connection between creator and audience. Your work tells a story, and so do you. These intertwined narratives elevate the cultural value of your creation.

Authenticity is the foundation of this law. People are naturally drawn to genuine stories, and when they understand the inspiration, struggles, or purpose behind your work, they feel a personal connection. It's not just the art or the product they admire; it's the human effort, vulnerability, and vision that make it resonate. The more your audience sees your humanity, the more loyalty and emotional investment they bring to your work.

The context of creation also imbues your work with additional meaning. A painting isn't just color on canvas when its story is known; it becomes a chronicle of the hours spent in careful strokes, the emotions infused into each hue, and the personal or societal circumstances that shaped it. The story transforms the work, elevating its significance and creating a shared experience between creator and audience. A work of art becomes more than itself; it becomes a vessel for connection.

Over time, the creator's narrative becomes inseparable from the work. This fusion builds a lasting legacy. Let's pay homage to Frida Kahlo. Her self-portraits are widely admired, but their true power lies in how they intertwine with her life story, her chronic pain, turbulent love, and cultural pride. Kahlo's openness about her struggles and triumphs amplifies the emotional resonance of her art. Today, her work and her narrative are celebrated as one, each enriching the other in the collective cultural memory.

In contemporary terms, Greta Gerwig's *Barbie* demonstrates the potency of sharing the creative narrative. As a feminist filmmaker, Gerwig openly discussed her intentions to balance humor with social critique, providing insight into her artistic choices. Her transparency framed *Barbie* as more than entertainment; the movie became a cultural conversation about gender and identity. By sharing her process and purpose, Gerwig ensured her narrative was inseparable from the film's impact.

Your process of creation is not a private act. Sharing your journey, its inspirations, struggles, and triumphs, invites audiences into your world. Reflect on your Why, and share it in ways that feel authentic. What drives you to create? What experiences have shaped your vision? This is not an indulgence; it is an extension of the creative act itself.

Documenting your process can also bring audiences closer. Behind-the-scenes glimpses provide context that enriches the audience's experience of the final work. These details make the creative process tangible and relatable, turning your audience into witnesses of your evolution.

To expand the reach of your narrative, consider how different platforms can tell different facets of your story. Social media, blogs, podcasts, and live events offer opportunities to connect with your audience in unique ways. Each platform allows you to highlight different elements of your journey, weaving a multidimensional narrative that complements your work.

Invite your audience to participate. Engagement transforms passive observers into active participants. Allow them to offer feedback, vote on creative decisions, or simply witness the unfolding of your ideas. This collaboration fosters deeper emotional investment and strengthens the bond between you and your audience.

The narrative of creation is an essential component of cultural impact. When audiences understand the story behind your work, they see not just the result but the humanity that created it. This connection elevates both the work and its creator, leaving an enduring legacy. By sharing your process, your purpose, and your journey, you ensure that your narrative becomes a vital part of the work's resonance and value.

85

LAW FOUR: CULTURE IS NOT GIVEN, IT IS DISCOVERED

True culture is not imposed from above; it is unearthed from below. The ideas and creations that resonate most deeply are not dictated by institutions or gatekeepers but are instead discovered, adopted, and championed by individuals and communities. Culture thrives when it feels personal, like an intimate secret waiting to be shared. When audiences feel they have found something on their own terms, it ceases to be merely consumed; it is owned, integrated, and treasured. This bottom-up dynamic is what gives culture its enduring power.

The act of discovery transforms passive observers into active participants. When someone stumbles upon a piece of music, art, or storytelling that speaks to them, the connection feels authentic and deeply personal. They weren't sold on it; they claimed it for themselves. This sense of ownership fuels passion and loyalty, turning casual audiences into devoted communities. It is not the scale of discovery that matters but its authenticity. A music fan who finds an unknown band through an obscure streaming platform often feels a stronger connection to that band than to a heavily marketed chart-topper. Discovery carries emotional weight.

The legitimacy of culture also emerges from its grassroots adoption. Cultural movements that rise organically often carry a resonance and loyalty that no top-down campaign can replicate. Jazz in the 1920s, for instance, began in the underground clubs and speakeasies of New Orleans. It was a product of the people, a symbol of rebellion, freedom, and emotional release. While elites dismissed or even tried to suppress it, their resistance only amplified its appeal. What began as a localized form of expression eventually redefined global music, a testament to the enduring power of grassroots cultural validation.

In contrast, attempts to impose culture from the top down frequently falter. When institutions, advertisers, or power structures try to dictate what should be celebrated, the result is often hollow and uninspired. Audiences reject what feels forced, preferring the freedom to explore and interpret on their own. The rise of platforms like TikTok exemplifies this dynamic in the modern era. On TikTok, creators bypass traditional gatekeepers to engage directly with audiences. Trends like Lil Nas X's *Old Town Road* grew not because they were decreed by an industry but because they were discovered, shared, and celebrated organically by users who felt like co-creators in their success.

Embracing this law requires humility and a shift in perspective. Your role is not to dictate but to inspire, to craft work that invites exploration rather than demands attention. Authenticity is your most powerful tool. Create from a place of honesty, staying true to your voice and vision rather than chasing fleeting trends or external expectations. The deeper your authenticity, the more resonant your work will be.

Instead of selling, focus on seeding. Share your work in places where discovery feels natural. A musician might upload their track to small platforms, allowing word-of-mouth to generate excitement before broader promotion. Similarly, an author might serialize stories on social-community platforms, creating a sense of discovery and fostering early advocates.

Engaging directly with grassroots communities amplifies this process. Small, passionate audiences are often the most vocal champions of new work. By responding to their feedback, engaging in conversations, and making them feel part of your journey, you deepen their connection and loyalty. Encourage participation wherever possible, whether you are a filmmaker releasing alternate endings for fans to debate or a designer inviting input on future collections. These opportunities for audience involvement transform your work into something shared rather than dictated.

Above all, embrace slow growth. Culture is not built overnight. It takes time for ideas to gain traction, for audiences to claim them as their own, and for movements to gather momentum. Rushing to force adoption can dilute the authenticity that makes your work meaningful in the first place. Patience allows your creations to find their natural audience, one that will value and sustain them over the long term.

Culture that resonates is never handed down; it is claimed, explored, and cherished by the audience. As a creator, your responsibility is not to impose but to inspire discovery. By staying authentic, inviting participation, and respecting the organic nature of cultural adoption, you ensure your work becomes a living part of the cultural fabric. True culture is not given; it is discovered. That discovery is what makes it endure.

86

LAW FIVE: TO INCITE EVANGELISTS, THERE MUST BE A GOSPEL

Word of mouth is the most potent force in cultural growth, but it is rarely spontaneous. For your creative work to inspire evangelists, those impassioned advocates who will spread the word, you must give them a gospel. This gospel is the story they will carry forth, a clear and compelling narrative that simplifies and amplifies their enthusiasm. People may love your work, but to share it with others, they need the language, the framing, and the tools to communicate that love. Without this, even the most passionate audience may falter, unsure of how to convey their excitement.

The mechanism of creating this gospel begins with clarity. If your message is muddy, convoluted, or overly complex, it will falter in translation. Evangelists need a concise, memorable way to describe your work—something as simple as an elevator pitch or tagline that distills its essence. You need to give it to them. For example, when Lin-Manuel Miranda first described *Hamilton*, he famously said, "It's the story of America then, told by America now." In one sentence, he encapsulated the project's historical gravity, modern relevance, and innovative approach. Such precision doesn't just make it easier to share; it makes it impossible to forget.

Emotional resonance is the next essential ingredient. Passionate advocacy arises when audiences feel something profound: joy, sorrow, wonder, outrage. Emotion is the spark that compels them to recommend your work to others. Consider the success of *Everything Everywhere All at Once* in 2022. The Daniels' genre-defying film dazzled with its visual inventiveness, and more: It struck a deeply emotional chord. Fans described how it made them laugh, cry, and reflect on life's infinite possibilities. The gospel of this film was its wild creativity plus its heartfelt message, a combination that made word-of-mouth unstoppable. And won it the Best Picture Academy Award.

Framing the story is equally vital. Your work might be brilliant, but without a narrative to contextualize its importance, it risks being overlooked. Audiences need to know why your work matters, what it stands for, and how it fits into the broader cultural moment. Martin Luther's *95 Theses*, for instance, sparked the Protestant Reformation not solely because of their theological arguments but because they were shared in a way that ignited personal and communal action. Luther's followers didn't merely read his words; they adopted his mission, spreading his ideas with fervor because they understood the stakes.

Ease of sharing cannot be overlooked. In the digital landscape, the tools you provide for your audience to spread the word can make or break your gospel. Memes, social media posts, short videos: These are the modern equivalents of Luther's printing press. When a piece of content is designed to be shareable, its reach multiplies exponentially. Think again of how Lil Nas X leveraged TikTok for *Old Town Road*. The song's gospel was catchy, irreverent, and endlessly remixable, allowing users to engage with it creatively. The result was a viral phenomenon that reshaped the music industry.

For creators, crafting a gospel for your work requires intention. Start by defining your core message: What is the simplest and most compelling way to describe what you've made? Reflect on the emotional resonance of your work and make it central to your narrative. Share your journey, the struggles and triumphs that shaped your creation, to give it depth and relatability. Provide your audience with tools to share—short clips, impactful visuals, a compelling phrase. Then, engage with your early evangelists. Amplify their voices by acknowledging their contributions, sharing their enthusiasm, and giving them an insider role in your creative journey.

People want to share what they love, and they need guidance and inspiration to do so effectively. Your gospel provides this, transforming passive admiration into active advocacy. Word of mouth is not about what you made. It's about the story people tell about your creation. By crafting a gospel that is clear, emotional, and shareable, you empower your audience to become your most powerful allies.

87

LAW SIX: SOCIAL PROOF SPIRALS OUTWARD

Creative work thrives on the energy of its most passionate supporters. At the center of any cultural phenomenon lies a devoted core—a group of white-hot fans whose enthusiasm radiates outward, attracting others and amplifying the work's reach. This ripple effect, known as social proof, is the engine of enduring cultural impact. It transforms individual admiration into collective momentum, with energy spiraling outward in an ever-expanding wave. This is not an accident; it's the result of understanding and cultivating the natural dynamics of human connection and enthusiasm.

Social proof begins with a devoted core. These fans are more than just admirers. They're validators. Their visible dedication signals to others that your work is worth noticing, engaging with, and celebrating. For example, the Grateful Dead's Deadheads, a core group of around 20,000 die-hard followers, didn't just attend concerts, they lived and breathed the music. They created a subculture that traveled with the band, taping shows, sharing recordings, and spreading the Dead's ethos organically. This grassroots fervor drew in millions of casual listeners, converting them into lifelong fans. The Dead's legacy wasn't built in arenas; it was born from the passion of a few and spiraled outward.

The power of social proof lies in its contagiousness. Superfans act as magnets. Their energy and excitement are palpable, making others curious and eager to join. Lady Gaga, in the early days of her career, understood this dynamic perfectly. At her concerts, she reserved prime seating for her "Little Monsters," ensuring they were at the center of the action. The intensity of their devotion inspired the rest of the audience, transforming casual listeners into loyal followers. Gaga's strategic focus on her core fans created an electrifying atmosphere that spiraled outward, growing her audience with every performance.

Participation fuels the spiral. Devoted fans don't just consume—they actively contribute to the culture around your work. They share, advocate, and even co-create, amplifying your reach without direct effort on your part. Beyoncé's BeyHive exemplifies this phenomenon. When she released *Lemonade*, her fans mobilized en masse, creating memes, sharing insights, and organizing watch parties. Beyoncé didn't need to push her work into the cultural conversation; her fans carried it there, driven by their deep connection to her artistry and message. Social proof spirals outward when fans are empowered to become participants in the creative journey.

For creators, harnessing the power of social proof requires forethought. Start by identifying and nurturing your core fans. Who are the people already championing your work? Engage with them directly, show your appreciation, and build a relationship. Exclusive experiences deepen this connection. Whether it's early access, private events, or personalized content, offering something special to your core fans reinforces their commitment and amplifies their enthusiasm.

Empowering fans to share your work is equally critical. Provide them with tools that make it easy for them to spread the word. Let them co-create the culture by encouraging fan art, fan fic, memes, or interpretations of your work. This participatory approach turns passive supporters into active evangelists, multiplying the impact of your efforts.

Visibility matters, too. Showcase your relationship with your core fans publicly. Repost their content, thank them in appearances and posts, acknowledge their contributions. This signals authenticity, inviting others to join the growing movement. Back in the day, the Grateful

Dead embraced this ethos by encouraging concert taping, understanding that fan-driven sharing would strengthen, not dilute, their cultural presence.

Your most devoted fans are the engine of your creative culture. Their passion validates your work, attracts new audiences, and creates a self-sustaining spiral of engagement. Social proof amplifies your energy. By cultivating this dynamic and giving your fans the tools to share their enthusiasm, that energy radiates far beyond what you could achieve alone. In the end, the ripple effects of social proof transform your audience into a community, your community into a movement, and your movement into enduring cultural impact.

88

LAW SEVEN: AWARENESS IS NOT DESIRE

Awareness is not desire. Just because people know your work exists doesn't mean they want to engage with it. This is a fundamental mistake in creative marketing: the assumption that visibility is enough. Awareness may put your work in front of an audience, but it does little to move them emotionally or compel them to act. In the movie business, we distinguish "awareness" from "want-to-see."

"Want-to-see" is what matters. "Want-to-see" is desire. Desire transforms passive recognition into active participation. It is curiosity, relevance, and emotional connection that spark genuine interest and propel your audience to engage.

Awareness alone is passive. A billboard might inform millions of people about a new movie, but without a compelling hook or emotional resonance, it becomes nothing more than visual noise. Advertisements and social media posts may alert people to a release date, but they fail if they don't generate a sense of urgency or intrigue. Desire, on the other hand, requires an emotional pull. It's what makes people feel they need to experience your work. A trailer that teases an intriguing storyline or introduces relatable characters stirs curiosity and sets the stage for deeper engagement.

Yet there's a fine balance. Oversaturation, too much awareness with too little substance, can backfire. It risks making the audience feel oversold, creating fatigue or skepticism. Excessive campaigns without meaningful content often lead to apathy or rejection. The audience doesn't just want to be told about your work; they want to be invited into a narrative that feels worth their time.

Consider the failures and successes of recent cultural phenomena. Sony's *Morbius* (2022) was marketed heavily, ensuring widespread awareness; yet the trailers lacked compelling storytelling, and early reviews dampened any potential intrigue. Audiences knew the movie existed, but they didn't feel motivated to see it. In contrast, Greta Gerwig's *Barbie* (2023) exemplified how to combine awareness with desire. The film's marketing hinted at stunning visuals and clever, satirical storytelling, sparking both curiosity and excitement. The result was a cultural moment that drove box office success. On the other hand, *Cats* (2019) stands as a cautionary tale: a big-budget adaptation that spent millions on visibility but created confusion and unease through its trailers, leading to one of the most infamous box office disasters of the decade. In the gaming universe, the release of Grand Theft Auto 6's trailer, a year before the game's actual release, was a paradigm of desire creation: It attracted 475 million views in the first twenty-four hours, making it the fastest-growing video game launch in internet history.

For creators, understanding the distinction between awareness and desire is critical. Desire comes from knowing your audience and crafting messages that resonate with their emotions and interests. It's about creating intrigue, leaving enough mystery to make them want more. Teasers, sneak peeks, and selective reveals allow your audience to engage their imagination, turning curiosity into anticipation.

Social proof is another powerful tool. Early reviews, testimonials, or audience reactions act as a collective voice, building excitement and validating the worth of your work. A band posting snippets of fan reactions from their latest show or a filmmaker sharing enthusiastic comments from a preview screening can transform interest into genuine enthusiasm.

Storytelling is the backbone of creating desire. Your marketing should tell a story as compelling as the work itself. A fashion designer might use behind-the-scenes footage to show the passion and craftsmanship behind their collection, or an author might reveal the personal journey that inspired their novel. These narratives forge connections, making your audience feel part of the process.

It's equally important to avoid overexposure. Saturating your audience with repetitive ads or constant reminders risks diminishing the appeal of your work. Instead, space your promotions and ensure each one adds value, whether it's highlighting a unique feature, showcasing a key moment, or providing new insights into your creation.

In the end, awareness opens the door, but desire is what brings people through it. Your work deserves more than passive acknowledgment. It deserves the active engagement of people who feel compelled to experience what you've created; enflamed with curiosity, suffused with emotion, their desire will lead them through your door.

89

LAW EIGHT: WITHOUT DISTRIBUTION, THERE IS NOTHING

Creative work only matters if it reaches an audience. Without effective distribution, even the most brilliant creations remain unseen, unappreciated, and unprofitable. Distribution is the backbone of creative industries. The companies that dominate music, movies, books, streaming, and gaming succeed not because they create the best art but because they have mastered the art of delivering work to audiences.

Accessibility determines impact. No matter how extraordinary a piece of creative work may be, it vanishes into obscurity if it cannot be accessed. An independent film that wins awards at festivals but has no streaming platform or theatrical release might as well not exist to the wider public. Accessibility transforms potential into presence. It makes creative work visible and viable.

Control of distribution equals control of culture. Companies that command distribution channels shape what audiences consume and, by extension, the cultural narratives that prevail. Streaming platforms like YouTube and Netflix use algorithms to determine what music or films are promoted, wielding immense power over what becomes popular and what fades into irrelevance. In this way, distribution is not just logistical, it is ideological, determining the cultural priorities of the moment.

Distribution multiplies value. A book sold in a single bookstore reaches a handful of readers, but the same book distributed globally in physical stores and digital platforms magnifies its reach exponentially. Effective distribution scales a creative work's impact, turning it from a local phenomenon into a global one.

Infrastructure becomes a competitive edge. Many of the world's most successful creative enterprises are fundamentally distribution companies. Amazon, for example, is as much a logistics powerhouse as it is a retailer, ensuring books, movies, and music are delivered to audiences everywhere. The ability to distribute efficiently and at scale often matters more than the content itself.

History offers clear evidence of the transformative power of distribution. The printing press revolutionized knowledge dissemination by replacing the painstaking process of handwritten manuscripts. This shift allowed works like Martin Luther's *95 Theses* and Shakespeare's plays to reach broad audiences, forever altering culture and society.

In contemporary times, Netflix has demonstrated how mastery of distribution can create dominance. Starting as a DVD rental company, it evolved into a global streaming service by focusing on how to deliver content seamlessly to viewers across devices and borders. Its success lies not just in the content it offers but in how effortlessly it reaches audiences. On the flip side, Taylor Swift's *Eras Tour* exposed the risks of poor distribution. Despite overwhelming demand, Ticketmaster's mishandling of ticket sales frustrated fans and caused reputational harm, proving that even extraordinary creative work is vulnerable to flawed delivery mechanisms.

For creatives, distribution must be part of the process from the beginning. Choosing the right channels is essential. Understanding where your target audience consumes creative work allows you to prioritize platforms that align with their preferences. Building relationships with distributors—publishers, streaming platforms, or other intermediaries—extends your reach. Multi-channel access maximizes your potential, offering audiences different ways to engage, whether through digital formats, physical editions, or experiential events.

Understanding algorithms is another critical skill. Distribution platforms use algorithms to decide what content rises to the top, making discoverability a key factor in success. Tailoring your work to digital visibility, optimizing for AI-semantic search, keywords, content accessibility, targeted marketing, will significantly amplify your reach. Above all, planning distribution early ensures that your work has a clear and strategic path to its intended audience.

Creative work without distribution is like a tree falling in the forest with no one around to hear it. The act of creating is incomplete without the act of sharing. To succeed, you must think not only as an artist but as a strategist, ensuring your work reaches the people it was made for. Perhaps content is king. But distribution is the Queen Mother.

90

LAW NINE: ABSOLUTE CONTROL IS IMPOSSIBLE

Once creative work leaves the artist's hands, it takes on a life of its own. No matter how much you refine, curate, or protect your vision, the moment your work enters the world, creative and emotional ownership begins to shift to the audience. This transfer of control is not a loss. It is an evolution. It ensures that your work continues to live and grow, shaped by interpretations, cultural contexts, and the imagination of others. To thrive as a creator, you must accept this reality: Absolute control is impossible.

Audiences redefine creative work. They bring their own emotions, experiences, and perspectives, often interpreting themes or messages in ways you never intended. A song about personal heartbreak might become an anthem for a movement, or a film might resonate for reasons far removed from its original intent. This reinterpretation is not a betrayal; it is proof of your work's power to connect and inspire.

Cultural and temporal shifts further transform meaning. A book written as satire for one era may become a prophetic critique in another. *The Great Gatsby*, for example, was a modest success in F. Scott Fitzgerald's time but later emerged as a defining critique of the American Dream, shaped by the evolving perspectives of readers and scholars. Creative work, like all cultural artifacts, is in constant dialogue with the world around it.

Audience engagement creates ownership. Fans extend creative works through memes, fan art, reinterpretations, and other derivative creations. While this can feel like a loss of control, it is evidence of deep resonance. George Lucas's *Star Wars* universe is a prime example. Initially crafted with a singular vision, the franchise has been shaped and expanded by fans who embraced it as their own, creating a subculture that sustains its relevance across generations.

Even during creation, control is an illusion. Time, money, materials, collaborators, and external forces all impose constraints that shape the final outcome. These limitations are not necessarily negative—they often inspire innovation and focus—but they remind us that no creative act exists in a vacuum.

Consider the constraints of time and resources. Deadlines dictate what can be achieved, as seen in Steven Spielberg's *Jaws.* Mechanical failures with the shark prop forced Spielberg to rely on suspenseful editing and music, creating a tension-filled masterpiece that might never have existed without those limitations. Similarly, Vincent van Gogh's limited access to materials influenced his bold colors and textures, which became hallmarks of his genius.

Collaboration further complicates control. Creative projects often involve teams, requiring negotiation and compromise. Christopher Nolan's films, while heavily shaped by his vision, reflect the superb contributions of cinematographers, composers, and studios. This interplay of perspectives enhances the work's richness, showing that control is not synonymous with quality or success.

Cultural and political forces also exert influence. During the McCarthy era, screenwriter Dalton Trumbo worked under pseudonyms to navigate censorship, while Chinese artist Ai Weiwei has repeatedly adapted his work to counter oppressive regimes. In my own work as a film producer, constraints come from the structures of the system itself, the power and authority of financiers, studios, and distributors to make or break a movie; my work is a perpetual dance within these boundaries. Constraints, though challenging, often fuel creativity and amplify the message behind the work.

The unexpected can alter the creative process in profound ways. Mechanical failures, last-minute changes, and accidental discoveries often lead to innovations that surpass the creator's original intent. These moments are reminders that creativity thrives not in the perfection of control but in the resilience to adapt.

To embrace the impossibility of absolute control is to embrace the full potential of creative work. Letting go allows your art to evolve, connect, and endure in ways beyond your imagination. It transforms your audience from passive observers to active participants, expanding the reach and relevance of your work.

Creative constraints, whether imposed by time, resources, collaborators, or culture, are not barriers; they are opportunities. By navigating imperfection with openness and innovation, you can create work that resonates more deeply, lives more fully, and transcends your initial vision. The beauty of creative work lies not in controlling its journey but in setting it free.

91

LAW TEN: BEAUTY AND MONEY ARE NOT MEASURES OF EACH OTHER, AND BEAUTY IS MORE ENDURING

Money measures success in the moment; beauty measures success across time. These two metrics rarely align. Some of the most enduring works of art and culture were created under financial strain or ignored commercially during their creators' lifetimes. Conversely, many blockbuster successes fade from memory as quickly as their profits are counted. For creatives, this reality is both grounding and liberating: You may chase money to sustain your craft, but the pursuit of beauty creates a legacy.

Beauty resides in emotional and spiritual resonance. It appeals to the soul, not the wallet. A beautiful work connects people through shared humanity, evoking emotions that endure far beyond the artist's time. By contrast, commercial value often responds to fleeting trends or market pressures. Consider Mozart's *Requiem*, which continues to move listeners with its haunting beauty centuries after his death. At the time of its creation, Mozart was struggling financially, but his work transcended his immediate circumstances to become timeless.

Commercial success is bound to the moment. The films, books, and songs that dominate box offices or charts are often products of their time, designed to cater to current tastes. Their financial rewards, while significant, rarely translate into enduring cultural value. Popular films, like most in the Marvel Cinematic Universe, achieve record-breaking revenue but often lack the lasting emotional and intellectual resonance of less commercially successful yet more artistically profound works. And in ten years, I doubt people will remember many MCU movies.

Money buys moments. Money can sustain your craft, providing the resources and stability to create, but it is beauty that grants your work immortality. Vincent van Gogh sold only a handful of paintings and never got recognition as an artist during his lifetime, yet his *Starry Night* is now one of the most celebrated and recognized works of art in the world. His single-focus pursuit of beauty, not profit, secured his place in history.

Even when money and beauty coexist, it is rare and unpredictable. Toni Morrison's novels, such as *Beloved*, were not best-seller hits upon release but have since become literary cornerstones, celebrated for their profound exploration of the human condition. Her work exemplifies how beauty's value accrues over time, often outlasting the economic systems that initially overlooked it.

The distinction between beauty and money challenges creatives to examine their motivations. Money is transactional and ephemeral, tied to specific moments and markets. Beauty, by contrast, is timeless. It transcends the creator and speaks to something universal, something that connects past, present, and future. To pursue beauty is to contribute something that lives on through the people it touches.

This understanding does not negate the necessity of financial realities. Creatives must navigate the balance between sustaining their lives and pursuing their art. Commercial work can fund the pursuit of beauty, just as beauty can give meaning to the grind of commercial endeavors. However, it is essential to remember that financial success, while helpful, is not the ultimate measure of creative worth.

Money is transient; beauty remains. As a creative, you walk the line between the fleeting demands of commerce and the enduring pursuit of meaning. When you prioritize beauty, you create for the Now and for all the Nows to come.

ENVOI

THE NATION AT THE END OF THE WORLD

Now the mantle shifts, from one to the other, a handing off of the baton.

We live at the end of one era. And the start of the next one.

We didn't know how long it would take, for the nation's interior to dissolve and reshape itself, but we felt it happening. Even in the short space of our time together, we have felt the changes becoming more pronounced.

It isn't easy to live with awareness today, to make our creative work in the face of shadow forces. As we have been on this journey together, in these pages, you and I, we've changed, too, and I believe our changes are microcosms of larger transformations.

Yes, it is hard. Yes, it is uncomfortable. Yes, it is also joyous, resolute, profound. Because our work matters. It becomes more significant as every minute passes.

Creative work is the defining act of leadership. Change does not come from the void. It comes from creative action that charts a course, sets a vision for what will be. Only then will people, companies, cultures, societies walk along the stones that narrative has set.

The state of the world now is crisis. Only creativity will lead us to renewal. To emerge into renewal, we will reengage our curiosity, empathy, and emotions. Which is what creative work does. Our experience of this life is not data-driven; it is based on our emotional responses to all around us, and creative works are the laboratories in which we learn about our emotions, experiment with them, discover what makes us feel joy or fear, and how we feel about that.

No single creative work can change the world. No single person can change the world. But the world does not change without art, without creative expression, without people sensitive to creative resonance.

We have our work to do. We have the imagination. We've got to show the way.

You, yes you, you reading these words, are here to do your work, to make your art, to make your difference. To persist so the difference may be made. To lean into your unique vision and express yourself, whatever it takes and in the way you do. To move through your fears so fearlessness may take hold.

I do not know what I do not know.

I do not know your beauties, your truths.

Show us.

ACKNOWLEDGMENTS

No work stands on its own. It has taken me decades to distill what's in these pages, and every relationship and experience has added to them. I thank every large organization I've been a part of, and the people who worked there—Los Angeles Actors' Theatre, Los Angeles Theatre Center, Walt Disney Studios, Interscope/PolyGram, National Geographic Society, UC Berkeley's Haas School of Business.

Every project, whether we got it made or not, has had its exceptional creative community: artists, writers, directors, producers, editors, actors, cinematographers, visual effects artists, sound designers, engineers, programmers, learning designers, marketers, distributors, accountants, technicians. Audiences don't stay for all the credits to roll, and the credit roll for this book would take hours; know that I am grateful to you all. Especially, my thanks to the early readers who generously gave perceptive notes and encouragement, and to Deborah Heimann for smart and sensitive copy editing, to Jaina Shaw for research and fact-checking, and to Geo Derice for shepherding this book through the publication process.

Some years ago, in a time of personal darkness, four friends metaphorically broke into the metaphoric cave I had sealed myself in and pulled me out. Sarah Ream, Ellen McLaughlin, Rinde Eckert, Robert Myhill and I began our own salon, staying in group houses in different parts of the world to support each other and our work. I started writing this book in one of those houses.

More recently, Angelica Rose Toumbas, who curates Rosemary's House, invited me to lead a writers' workshop perched on a cliff overlooking the Aegean. The experience brought me to finish this book.

My children, Chloe and Amara, now grown and living their own expressive lives, making positive change in their communities and the world, inspire me every day. As do my grandchildren, who will forge paths of their own.

Dominique and I fell in love within hours of meeting each other—a story for another book. The world knows Dominique Shelton Leipzig as a world-class advisor and celebrated attorney seeking to hardcode humanity into AI and empowering business and government leadership to do so. I know her as the most generous, supportive, selfless, trustworthy, fun, and outspoken person. I measure my good fortune every day. There's no one I'd rather be in a foxhole with.

ABOUT THE AUTHOR

Adam Leipzig has done a lot of things, but he describes himself simply as a curious person, whose curiosity has walked him along many roads. Adam's work focuses on quality and profitable international media built on strong business fundamentals; establishing supportive opportunities for content creators; and sharing skills and knowledge to expand access and careers for upcoming generations. He has worked with more than ten thousand creative artists in film, theater, television, music, dance, poetry, literature, performance, photography, and design.

Adam was the first American theater dramaturg outside of New York City. In the performing arts, he has produced more than three hundred plays and other events, including the first plays by Donald Freed, David Henry Hwang, Joyce Carol Oates, steve carter, and Jon Robin Baitz; work by avant-garde theater troupe Mabou Mines; the theater experiences of Reza Abdoh; music with Tito Puente, Cab Calloway, Jan Garbarek, and Richard Stoltzman; and dance with Sarah Elgart.

As senior executive at Walt Disney Studios, president of National Geographic Films, and working independently, Adam has been a producer, distributor, or supervising executive on thirty-nine films that have disrupted expectations, including *March of the Penguins*; *Honey, I Shrunk the Kids*; *Dead Poets Society*; *Titus*; *The Way Back*; *A Plastic Ocean;* and *Sicilian Holiday.* Adam's movies have won or been nominated for 10 Academy Awards, 11 BAFTA Awards, 2 Golden Globes, 2 Emmys, 2 Directors Guild Awards, 4 Sundance Awards and 4 Independent Spirit Awards. Collectively, his projects have generated over $2 billion in revenue on $300 million production spending, and twice he has been responsible for the "most profitable film of the year."

Adam serves as professional faculty at the Haas School of Business, University of California, Berkeley, where he teaches in both the MBA and Executive Education programs. He is the author of two previous books, *Filmmaking in Action*, and *Inside Track for Independent Filmmakers.*

Adam publishes the popular digital magazine *Cultural Daily*, a curated forum for culture and creativity, which has published more than 4,000 writers, including 1,500 poets; and *DCReport*, a nonprofit investigative news and perspective service.

www.AdamLeipzig.com

www.ingramcontent.com/pod-product-compliance
Lightning Source LLC
LaVergne TN
LVHW101320110826
845152LV00016B/161/J

* 9 7 8 0 9 8 8 5 3 4 2 3 0 *